PRAISE FOR *PRINCIPAL RECRUITMENT AND RETENTION: BEST PRACTICES FOR MEETING THE CHALLENGES OF TODAY*

"The importance of principal leadership for the success of schools has been well-documented in international literature. At the same time, many schools worldwide have been struggling to recruit qualified principals and retain them in the job. This book brings highly relevant and exciting cases from various national contexts together and expands the current knowledge base on the recruitment and retention of school principals. I want to congratulate the editors and authors for their great effort to provide such a guiding source for educational leaders and policymakers around the world."

—**Sedat Gümüş**, associate professor, The Education University of Hong Kong, Hong Kong, SAR

"Recruiting and retaining talented principals is certainly a big challenge in schools in the New York metropolitan area. Research is axiomatic. Schools need talented principals, efforts need to be enhanced to attract the very best, and programs and practices need to be implemented to encourage retention. *Principal Recruitment and Retention* is an important addition to the literature. Each chapter explores these issues with a grounding in extant research in the field with practical suggestions that will be helpful to many schools and districts. The editors did a marvelous job recruiting a diverse cadre of contributors."

—**Susan Sullivan**, College of Staten Island, City University of New York

BRIDGING THEORY AND PRACTICE

Series Editor: Jeffrey Glantz

Bridging Theory and Practice is an international series on school leadership that reflects the latest cutting-edge theories and practice in school leadership. The series motto is framed after Kurt Lewin's famous statement, paraphrased, that there is no sound theory without practice, and no good practice that is not framed on some theory. Authors in this series illustrate the intimate and integral connection between the two divides.

Books In Series

Regenerating Education as a Living System: Success Stories of Systems Thinking in Action edited by Kristen M. Snyder and Karolyn J. Snyder

Bridging Leadership and School Improvement: Practical Strategies for Improving Teaching and Learning by Leslie Ann Locke and Sonya D. Hayes

Principal Recruitment and Retention: Best Practices for Meeting the Challenges Today edited by Chanina Rabinowitz and Michael Reichel

Actionable Feedback to PK–12 Teachers edited by Alyson L. Lavigne and Mary Lynne Derrington

Systems Thinking for Sustainable Schooling: A Mindshift for Educators to Lead and Achieve Quality Schools edited by Karolyn J. Snyder and Kristen M. Snyder

For a complete list of books in the Bridging Theory and Practice series, please see https://rowman.com/Action/SERIES/_/RLBTP/Bridging-Theory-and-Practice

Principal Recruitment and Retention

Best Practices for Meeting the Challenges of Today

Edited by
Chanina Rabinowitz
Michael Reichel

ROWMAN & LITTLEFIELD
Lanham • Boulder • New York • London

Published by Rowman & Littlefield
An imprint of The Rowman & Littlefield Publishing Group, Inc.
4501 Forbes Boulevard, Suite 200, Lanham, Maryland 20706
www.rowman.com

86-90 Paul Street, London EC2A 4NE, United Kingdom

Copyright © 2023 by Chanina Rabinowitz and Michael Reichel

All rights reserved. No part of this book may be reproduced in any form or by any electronic or mechanical means, including information storage and retrieval systems, without written permission from the publisher, except by a reviewer who may quote passages in a review.

British Library Cataloguing in Publication Information Available

Library of Congress Cataloging-in-Publication Data

Names: Rabinowitz, Chanina, 1954- editor. | Reichel, Michael, 1969- author.
Title: Principal recruitment and retention : best practices for meeting the challenges today / edited by Chanina Rabinowitz and Michael Reichel.
Description: Lanham, Maryland : Rowman & Littlefield, 2023. | Series: Bridging theory and practice | Includes bibliographical references and index. | Summary: "This book will confront the difficult situation of principal recruitment and retention across several leading countries around the world"—Provided by publisher.
Identifiers: LCCN 2023004136 (print) | LCCN 2023004137 (ebook) | ISBN 9781475866483 (cloth) | ISBN 9781475866490 (paperback) | ISBN 9781475866506 (epub)
Subjects: LCSH: School principals—Recruiting—Case studies. | School principals—Selection and appointment—Case studies. | School principal turnover—Prevention—Case studies.
Classification: LCC LB2831.94 .P75 2023 (print) | LCC LB2831.94 (ebook) | DDC 371.2/012—dc23/eng/20230224
LC record available at https://lccn.loc.gov/2023004136
LC ebook record available at https://lccn.loc.gov/2023004137

Contents

Acknowledgments   vii

Series Editor's Introduction   ix
   Jeffrey Glanz

Editor's Introduction   xi
   Chanina A. Rabinowitz

Chapter 1: A Systematic Review of the Literature on Principal Recruitment: Best Practices   1
   Dustin W. Miller and Belinda Gimbert, The Ohio State University

Chapter 2: Principal Recruitment in New Zealand: The Role of Boards of Trustees   17
   Gülay Erin Dalgıç, University of Auckland

Chapter 3: Solving the Shortage of Principals in Israel by Recruiting Anglo Former Principals   31
   Michael Reichel, Michlalah Jerusalem College, Israel

Chapter 4: Strengthening Educational Leadership Preparation Programs to Better Prepare Principals to Aid Retention   43
   Kathleen M. W. Cunnigham, Henry Tran, Suzy Hardie, Tammy S. Taylor, and Renice K. Sauls, University of South Carolina

Chapter 5: We're Hiring, but Will They Come?: The Challenges of Recruiting Racially Diverse Principal Candidates in Rural Schools   57
   Simone A. F. Gause, Coastal Carolina University, Henry Tran, University of South Carolina and David G. Buckman, Augusta University

Chapter 6: Retaining Principals: What Works Best? 69
Belinda Gimbert and Dustin W. Miller, The Ohio State University

Chapter 7: Who Wants to Be a Principal?: Recruiting Instructional Leaders 85
Haim Shaked, Hemdat College of Education, Sdot Negev, Israel

Chapter 8: Challenges Facing Principals: Voices From the Field 97
David Scanga and Renee Sedlack, Saint Leo University

Chapter 9: Initiatives to Support Principals in the Early Years of their Careers 109
Shmuel Shenhav, Michlalah Jerusalem College

Chapter 10: A Proposal to Enhance Retention of School Principals in Türkiye 125
Pınar Ayyıldız, Ankara Medipol University and Köksal Banoğlu, Turkish Ministry of National Education

Index 139

About the Editors and Contributors 141

Acknowledgments

I would like to acknowledge the contributors of this volume who were impressively cooperative as we worked together. Thanks are extended to Michael Reichel, my co-editor, for his professional and congenial collaboration. It has been a pleasure working with Professor Jeffrey Glanz, who helped us keep up the momentum. Mostly, I thank my wife, Chana, for her willingness to let me dedicate the time to this project. I hope this work will help recruit and retain the best and brightest principals, whose influence is unparalleled in the effort to improve our schools.

—Chanina Rabinowitz

I wish to express my gratitude to Professor Jeffrey Glanz, Series Editor, for his encouragement, guidance, and support in bringing this work to fruition. Special thanks to Dr. Chanina Rabinowitz, my competent co-editor, for his untiring efforts throughout the editing process. I wish to thank my family for their support and encouragement throughout my decades in education. I am most grateful to my devoted wife, Atara, for all her encouragement and support during this project.

—Michael Reichel

Series Editor's Introduction

Jeffrey Glanz

A word about the current book in the Bridging Theory and Practice series: *Principal Recruitment and Retention*, competently edited by Chanina Rabinowitz and Michael Reichel, two former principals themselves.

Each chapter in this volume echoes the same messages: 1) the importance of the principalship in fostering and sustaining excellent schools, 2) a need to re-examine ways we recruit principals, and 3) to develop creative ways to retain these vital leaders.

In the late 1960s into the 70s, I recall a short-lived movement or rally cry to eliminate the principal position because, after all, teachers can go it alone, or hiring a business officer to run logistical operations was all that was needed. Some schools indeed experimented with these seemingly creative, avant-garde ideas. It wasn't too long that educators, the public, and even the progenitors of these experiments realized the folly of eliminating the principalship.

Ensuing research in the field undergirded the import of the principalship. Here are some selected highlights of this early research:

- The principal is *the* key player in the school building to promote student learning. It's not that students cannot learn without a principal for teachers are certainly most essential as front-line educators in the classroom. But, a specially-prepared instructional leader serving as building principal (or head of school) is vital in order to accomplish deep, sustained, and school-wide achievement for all students.
- High achievement for all students should be the major goal for a principal. A principal may possess charisma, increase parental participation in school activities, raise funds for the PTA, interact well with the Board, organize meaningful cultural events, or even possess great vision.

However, the bottom line is that a principal first and foremost should be concerned in activities that actively promote good teaching that in turn promotes student learning. A principal cannot be considered successful unless high student achievement in academic areas is achieved for all students.
- Although various forms of principal leadership (i.e., cultural, managerial, human resources, strategic, external development, and micropolitical) are important responsibilities, research demonstrates that the principal plays an active and orchestrating role in each.
- The effective principal is knowledgeable and skillful in the art and science of instructional supervision and leadership.

Having affirmed the importance of the principalship, research in the field grappled with varied ideas of attracting competent individuals to assume the vital position. Various criteria were highlighted (not to be reviewed here) and the role of schools of education was discussed in order to prepare stellar candidates. Alternative recruiting efforts also emerged in the literature. An additional, vital factor became readily apparent as research efforts into the principalship continued. Principals seemed to be overburdened with a plethora of responsibilities. Research in the field began exploring ways of retaining competent principals and minimizing the stressors and strains that led to a high attrition rate among principals

Various plans and proposals were developed and implemented with uneven success. Today, well into the 21st century, the subject of recruiting and retaining excellent principals remains a grave concern. This volume brings current thinking into focus from an international perspective. Quite honestly, I cannot claim that this volume will end the discussion on the topic, but it will certainly raise innovative ideas and practices from a multi-dimensional perspective.

All comments may be sent to the individual contributors, co-editors, and/or the series editor. We hope this new volume in the Bridging Theory and Practice series will bring fresh ideas to improve the recruitment and retention of principals, who are so vital to successful schooling.

Editor's Introduction

Chanina A. Rabinowitz

Principal Recruitment and Retention: Best Practices for Meeting the Challenges Today presents the latest theories and practices aimed at addressing global challenges. This book will find great relevance to boards or ministries of education, school district leaders, school board members, and state and regional policymakers.

Principals and their aspirants will also find much value in the concepts and ideas presented by a group of talented and diverse contributors. The book is certainly valuable for its authors' contributions, as the authors are from a broad range of institutions that prepare individuals for the principalship. Beyond the inevitable challenges involved in recruiting and retaining school leaders, the ideas expressed will help practitioners navigate seemingly intractable problems and issues associated with the principalship.

Two contributions of *Principal Recruitment and Retention* set this book apart from others. First, we present the wisdom of theoreticians with a keen eye on praxis. True to the theme of the Rowman & Littlefield School Leadership Series, our book bridges theory with practice in attempting to highlight new ideas for recruiting and retaining principals. Second, this volume has an international flavor. Significant research from the United States, Türkiye, Israel, and New Zealand are represented in this volume and provide interesting insights that are applicable globally.

The book is fundamentally premised on the reciprocal relationship between recruitment and retention. Recruitment is unlikely to be successful if there is even a perception that most principalships are short-lived. Strengthening retention efforts aids principal recruitment.

Recruitment efforts, too, are dependent on strategic, ongoing, and meaningful programs (such as induction and mentoring) that are established to aid in retention. Due to this almost symbiotic relationship, *Principal Recruitment and Retention* presents extant scholarship coupled with practical strategies for both recruiting and retaining principals.

Reflecting upon and extending analysis of the relationship between recruitment and retention, a fundamental conundrum becomes readily apparent. The job of a principal is often fraught with overwhelming obstacles. A prominent obstacle reported by incumbent principals is that within the increased accountability movement that has characterized schooling over the past few decades, there have been increased pressures placed on teachers and especially principals to measure success primarily on student performance on achievement and other such standardized tests.

Moreover, principals work long and hard hours that consequently impact the delicate balance of work and life. Would-be principal candidates are aware of these increased pressures and responsibilities as well as added political complications, especially due to activist parents who insist on changes beyond their legitimate scope of influence. Salary, too, is often not commensurate with the excessive demands.

Several of the chapters allude to and amplify these challenges. Additional chapters highlight other issues. For instance, the principal recruitment process is generally spearheaded by the local school board. Not all school board members may be prepared for this process. Expert advice can better prepare them and to move the recruitment process forward.

Once on the job, a strong, trusting relationship is needed between the new hire and the school board. Several chapters discuss the need for boards and principals to develop trusting relationships based on openness, transparency, and clarity about each other's roles and responsibilities. This trust will lead to the principal's job satisfaction and accomplishments that will ripple throughout the school and district. Ultimately, students will be the beneficiaries of this trust and cooperation.

The challenges do not stop at the hiring stage. Principal neophytes need support through induction and mentoring, as is beginning to happen today. Principals who experience difficulties in describing or implementing their plans for the improvement of instruction, for example, should be equipped with a mentor through the first few difficult years of employment.

These themes and ideas are echoed by the contributors of this volume. In Chapter 1, Dustin Miller and Belinda Gimbert focus on extant research about principal recruitment. They summarize the strategies that are commonly used by school districts and suggest alternative methods that might be used to attract the "best and brightest" into the principalship. Recommendations are provided for incentives and other methods of recruiting candidates. These are especially important for districts that find it difficult to attract worthy and assorted candidates. Alternative methods for recruitment of identified aspirants are highlighted.

In Chapter 2, Gülay Erin Dalgıç analyzes the role of boards of trustees in the recruitment and appointment of principals in New Zealand. A critical review of practices and procedures to assure suitable principal appointments is presented. The author continues with a review of the initiatives taken by the New Zealand government to support boards of trustees in the appointment process and makes recommendations for improving this process. Governmental interventions have bred good results as the principals report positive relationships with their boards. Some of the responsibilities of each side are discussed. The suggestions offered are relevant for recruiting principals all over the world.

In Chapter 3, Michael Reichel, coeditor of this volume, reports on a study he conducted of school principals from English-speaking countries who resigned their positions and immigrated to Israel. He sees them as a treasure-chest of talent and experience that could be shared with children and schools in their new home country. This is an important step toward solving the principal shortage, at least in metropolitan areas of Israel. The positions available outnumber the candidates available; this problem requires immediate attention. Of course, these senior administrators would need acclimation into the Israeli educational system, but Reichel suggests a program that would support both the schools and the new school heads. He also delineates the orientation program that would be necessary for professional development of the new recruits.

In Chapter 4, scholars Kathleen M. W. Cunningham, Henry Tran, Suzy Hardie, Tammy S. Taylor, and Rinice K. Sauls presuppose that principal retention requires strong university-based educational leadership preparation programs together with in-service induction support. Because principal turnover is so maladaptive for schools, their staffs and students, they offer suggestions on what the preparation program should look like, and they identify its goals: for principals to feel success, self-efficacy, and growth in their roles. They argue that this will assure, as much as possible, that principals remain in their positions as they offer their schools effective leadership. When the multiple characteristics they describe are used collectively, future leaders will be adaptive to their contexts, communities, needs, and challenges. Specific suggestions are made for the curriculum of a successful preparation program.

Chapter 5 deals with the critical theme of diversity in the principal's role. Today we know that students learn better and enhance their social and emotional development when they see similar school leaders and teachers similar to them, such as from the same ethnic group. We also know that racially matched teachers and school leaders are more satisfied with their jobs and experience less turnover. However, 90% of rural American schools host White principals, such that the need to recruit diverse ethnic principals is important but difficult to achieve. Simone A. F. Gause, Henry Tran, and David Buckman offer recommendations for increasing diversity in school leadership. They also identify four obstacles to recruiting diverse candidates, explain these obstacles so that we might overcome them, and help school districts diversify their staffs.

Belinda Gimbert and Dustin Miller return in Chapter 6 to share their insights regarding principal retention. Stability is improved when policymakers implement practices that limit the stress of the position, offer stable and adequate compensation, allocate enough authority for decision-making and influence over school employees, and maintain unblurred work-life boundaries. Other factors include assuring the principal's sense of achievement from their intense efforts as well as collegial relationships with all school and community constituents. Involving parents in a positive way can enhance the school climate and ensure the principal's desire to stay. Offering specific quality professional mentoring and continued development will bolster the tenure of even experienced leaders.

Haim Shaked focuses on the importance of principals as instructional leaders. In Chapter 7, he discusses why it is so difficult to recruit principals who can demonstrate instructional leadership and what can be done to overcome this difficulty. Shaked writes that most principals lack the expertise to be instructional leaders and those who have it don't want to give up the classroom. He suggests we create a reality in which accepting a principalship, though a turn in the career path, allows one to continue teaching, but with the added leverage of having a broad impact on the academic accomplishments of the school. This approach, he says, is a way to bring those who love teaching and facilitating learning to school leadership positions.

In Chapter 8, David Scanga and Renee Sedlack analyze five topics that are challenging for principals. These surfaced from three major studies and include (1) instructional leadership, (2) autonomy, (3) feeling isolated and overwhelmed with responsibilities, (4) capacity building for teachers and staff, and (5) building trusting relationships. These "voices from the field" are important for district personnel and policymakers to hear. For example, principals yearn for autonomy so that they make the decisions that are right for their community, regardless of what other school leaders are doing. When central office leaders give dedicated principals this freedom, they grant them validation that helps incumbents retain their positions and makes recruitment easier and more effective.

In our penultimate chapter, Shmuel Shenhav offers critiques of pre-service preparation programs that have theoretical and practical components but are unattached to a principal's professional world. He suggests that principals should be hired based on their years of experience in educational settings and their completion of a recognized principal preparation curriculum. Then they should enter the school in which they have been selected principal and begin intensive work with a mentor as they face real challenges and actual dilemmas. Shenhav proposes a new kind of mentoring, one that guides the novice principal during the first two or three years of service, involving one-on-one support, and then continues through the induction period during years three to five, resulting in an alignment between preparation, mentoring, and induction that improves the recruitment and retention of school principals.

Our final chapter takes us to Türkiye to learn about issues of retention. There, too, the removal of a principal can be disruptive to the school climate and steady improvement. Türkiye is different in that its educational system is centralized, with little autonomy available to individual schools. This is significant when inexperienced candidates are presented for new openings. Pinar Ayyildiz and Köksal Banoğlu articulate a plan to help successful principals remain in their positions of leadership. This calls for improvements in Türkiye's pre-service and professional development programs, better working conditions, and proper compensation. They raise the question whether school leaders are born or nurtured into the position, something all mentors should consider. They share insights on retention in general and remediation when retention is uncertain.

Taken as a whole, *Principal Recruitment and Retention* offers traditional as well as innovative ideas to recruit and retain principals. Readers are encouraged to correspond with contributors to deepen the conversation about recruitment and retention of principals. Their email addresses are included in the book and we, and they, welcome your feedback and participation.

Chapter 1

A Systematic Review of the Literature on Principal Recruitment

Best Practices

Dustin W. Miller and Belinda Gimbert,
The Ohio State University

Recruitment is the "act of finding or adding new people to an organization or supporting a cause" (Merriam-Webster, n.d.). This could be lighthearted, such as recruiting a sibling to help convince parents that a vacation at the ocean would be better than hiking in the mountains. Or it could be professionally important, such as the recruitment of a world-renowned physician to practice at a top-tier medical center. Simply stated, recruitment is working to find the best possible person to do the job.

Interestingly, the concept of recruitment is not often associated with the hiring of K–12 education professionals. Superintendents, as chief executive officers, are sometimes recruited by search firms to lead school districts (Chion Kenney, 2003; Kamler, 2009), but the bulk of hires within education consist primarily of interested individuals applying for open positions.

Even with concerted efforts to bolster recruitment, evidence that the education profession prioritizes hiring through recruitment remains scant (Cieminski, 2018; Lee & Mao, 2020; Myung et al., 2011). To that end, it is the focus of this chapter to specifically review what is known about principal recruitment. How do school districts approach the recruitment of principals? What strategies are commonly used? And are there alternative methods to help school districts attract the best and brightest into the important role of the principalship?

To better understand the state of principal recruitment in K–12 education, we synthesized literature as a method of inquiry (Creswell, 2014) to discover what is known from studies of principal recruitment, primarily conducted between 2000 and 2021. A few works were uncovered and referenced prior to 2000, but most of our focus remains during the 21st century.

As a literature review, most of the information provided in this chapter is supported by empirical study. However, some content is not as heavily cited but, based on our collective professional experiences, is known as common practice throughout K–12 education. With this in mind, we attempted to strike a balance between what is known through empirical works versus common practices that have yet to be researched.

The following questions guided this search:

- Why is principal recruitment necessary in K–12 education?
- Are there deterrents to the use of recruiting to attract principals?
- What do we know about principal recruitment methods?
- Are alternative methods used to recruit principals?

We conducted an extensive literature search, applying a snowballing methodology (Somekh & Lewin, 2005) that allowed us to discover saturation between articles (Creswell, 2014). Although no literature review is ever exhaustive, acknowledging saturation served as a checkpoint to ensure that major gaps were not overlooked. Due to the K–12 education focus on principal recruitment, we limited our search to articles published in the English language and primarily included studies of early childhood to secondary principals in the United States or other developed nations.

THE PRINCIPALSHIP: SHOULD WE STAY OR SHOULD WE GO?

The school principalship is arguably one of the most important jobs in K–12 education and ranks second only to teachers in its positive impact on student learning (Pounder & Merrill, 2001; Seashore Louis et al., 2010). However, this critical position continues to be plagued by applicant shortages (Loeb et al., 2010; Snodgrass Rangel, 2018), early resignations (Lee & Mao, 2020; Stark-Price et al., 2006), pressures around student performance (Hancock et al., 2006), and poor work-life balance (Pounder & Merrill, 2001; Winter et al., 2002).

Principals continue to have increased responsibilities and are charged with making difficult decisions, while feeling the added political pressure to assuage angry community stakeholders when those decisions are not amenable to them (Cieminski, 2018; Pounder & Merrill, 2001; Zepeda et al., 2012). Equally problematic, the increased responsibility of school principals has outpaced the increase of administrator salaries (Kearney, 2010; Pijanowski et al., 2009; Wood et al., 2013). Even though educational leaders exhibit a sense of altruism in their approach, why should principals assume increased time, responsibility, and additional stress when their salaries remain comparable to those of teachers?

These issues are also problematic through the eyes of current educators. Teachers witness firsthand how principals have stressful jobs and work long hours, but often do not earn substantially more in comparison to the educators in their buildings. This creates a significant lack of incentive for teachers to assume the principalship (Lee & Mao, 2020; Whitaker, 2003).

In contrast to positioning the principalship as suffering from applicant shortages, studies have shown that the field is flush with possible candidates (Davis, 2005; National Association of Secondary School Principals, 1998; Zepeda et al., 2012), and the number of certified candidates continues to be almost double the number of leadership positions open each year (Gajda & Militello, 2008; Pijanowski et al., 2009; Roza, 2003). Although more recent studies have not been conducted, this poses an interesting question as to why teachers appear to be initially interested in earning administrative licenses, but then ultimately do not assume the principalship.

One could argue that there are simply not enough positions available for the volume of interested individuals or, as mentioned above, that the deleterious factors (i.e., long hours, stress, lack of financial incentive) are discouraging interested individuals from applying at all. This underscores a need to better understand how principal recruitment methods are being utilized and what we know about strategies to attract candidates to this valuable role.

PLANNING: A KEY FIRST STEP

According to Castetter and Young (2003), strong job candidates are generally not seeking new employment. When seeking talent, it is imperative to first devise a plan and utilize effective recruitment methods to secure a strong pool of applicants. Succession planning, a process used to predict job openings, can assist organizations in understanding future needs and how to prepare to fill leadership roles (Rothwell, 2010).

Understanding that the transition of a school leader is a stressful time when teachers can sense a range of emotions (Hargreaves & Fink, 2006), succession planning can help alleviate undue stress and offer an alternative to addressing shortages or challenges and finding suitable applicants (Cieminski, 2018). As

Lawler and Boudreau (2009) explain, people matter and organizations that prioritize talent need to be thoughtful about recruiting the best and brightest.

This process begins with a recruitment strategy that involves 1) a strategic plan to capture and fulfill the mission of the school district, 2) a projection of needs, 3) an audit of current staff, and 4) a vision (or profile) of the ideal candidates to meet those needs (Odden, 2011; Tomal & Schilling, 2018). Focusing on a recruitment strategy is the initial step K–12 school districts should prioritize to gain and cultivate strong candidates, both teachers and school leaders.

Development of a Strategic Plan

Strategic plans are a common tool used in K–12 education by school administrators to support high levels of student learning (McCarthy, 2015; McDonnell, 2012), but often these plans overlook the critical step of assessing human capital (Joseph, 2009). Strategic plans need to include hiring of top-notch talent, in all aspects of K–12 education (Odden, 2011; Tomal & Schilling, 2018). This includes principals. As the leaders of their schools, their ability to serve as strong leaders impacts the ability of teachers to, in turn, do what they need to on behalf of student learning (Hargreaves, 2009). A strategic plan that includes key steps that build toward student achievement can then serve as a roadmap for all key stakeholders.

Projection of Need

Depending on the location of a school district, growth, declining enrollment, or maintaining the status quo can be common realities. Understanding the direction of student enrollment is significant to preparing an effective recruitment strategy (Tomal & Schilling, 2018). If enrollment is increasing, how much staffing will be needed? Projecting need in advance allows for a thoughtful preparation for future hiring.

Not planning leaves a school district hiring at the last minute or relying on the application pool of any given season. Districts can use internal personnel to audit enrollment projections or engage with outside professional consulting firms. Regardless, it is key for recruitment planning to include student enrollment projections that frame future job needs.

Audit of Current Staff

The third step entails an audit of current staff. As Collins (2001) describes, it is not only important to have people on the bus, but also imperative to have them in the right seat on the bus. All too often, personnel are misplaced and continue to be ineffective in their roles. This is not healthy for any organization, but it is extremely harmful in K–12 education due to the nature of educating students. Odden (2011) frames a three-step process for conducting teacher talent audits. This process starts by making sure that all teachers are licensed to teach in the roles they currently hold. The second step consists of a review of past evaluations. Are these individuals performing? If not, have improvement plans been implemented to curb poor performance?

The third stage includes using formal data to gauge effectiveness (e.g., value-added, state tests results, surveys). The same process should be applied to principals. School principals should be adequately trained and/or licensed in their roles (Cieminski, 2018; Kearney, 2010; Roza, 2003), be evaluated for effectiveness (Grissom et al., 2019), and produce data-driven results that demonstrate how effective they are in leading student learning in their buildings.

Creating a Profile of a Principal

The final piece of a recruitment strategy is to establish a profile of a principal (Tomal & Schilling, 2018). This should not be a vision that is established in isolation from the superintendent or human resources department. School principals represent students, teachers, parents, and other members of their school community. Because of this, stakeholders from each of these focus groups should have a chance to discuss the attributes of their ideal principal (Richardson et al., 2016). This focus group information can then be used to develop a profile for the school principal. Not only can this profile be used to craft job descriptions, but it also provides a useful tool that positions new principal hires for success as they begin their work.

The process serves as a community building exercise by allowing key stakeholders to feel part of their schools by engaging in the important work of creating a profile of a principal. Once these pieces are in place, school districts are positioned to understand not only their need but also the profile of the best candidates to recruit for the principalship. With a developed recruitment strategy, the actual work of recruitment can begin.

METHODS OF RECRUITMENT

Methods focused on understanding principal recruitment continue to be rare (Lee & Mao, 2020; Stark-Price et al., 2006; Winter et al., 2002). However, there are strategies used to recruit principals, which generally mirror those of teacher recruitment, throughout the profession (Cieminski, 2018; Myung et al., 2011). The following methods will be discussed in this section:

considering employee referrals, using technology to post jobs, attending job fairs and partnering with local universities, and using incentives to attract candidates.

These methods apply a blend of active and inactive recruitment methods. Ideally, school districts should be working to actively attract candidates, but more common strategies rely on candidates noticing a posted position and applying. Inactive methods leave school districts vulnerable to who applies, but they still serve as an important form of principal recruitment.

Consider Employee Referrals

Employee referrals are a common recruitment strategy, especially from those working in the same school district (Tomal & Schilling, 2018). Principal openings are generally announced in advance, which provides teachers an opportunity to spread the word to colleagues and friends who may be interested. The institutional relationship between the teacher and school district gives a level of credibility to the employee referral.

This form of referral can also come as school leaders utilize their professional networks in the field to notify interested parties that a principalship is open. Again, a level of trust among colleagues can increase an applicant's credibility from the beginning of the process. This grassroots process can provide timely insight about the specific needs of the position, sought after skills and traits, and institutional knowledge about the school in need of a new principal.

The employee referral process has merit and is often utilized as an easy, no cost recruitment tool (Tomal & Shilling, 2018). Unfortunately, this recruitment strategy can harbor potential blind spots as well. Professionals tend to run in like-minded circles, which could limit the possibility of new thinking (Agosto & Roland, 2018). Additionally, this process can also minimize or exclude the potential to attract diverse candidates (Loeb et al., 2010; Thornton et al., 2022).

As K–12 student bodies continue to become more diverse (Grissom et al., 2017; Myung et al., 2011), it is important that teachers and principals mirror the diversity of their student bodies (Hill et al., 2016; Thornton et al., 2022; Lee & Mao, 2020). Relying heavily on employee referral can unintentionally produce more of the same.

Use Technology to Post Jobs

Traditional job postings are another form of recruitment (Tomal & Schilling, 2018; Winter & Morgenthal, 2002). A school district's posting of a job is the official, outward-facing call for interested candidates to apply. The information presented within the job posting, often referred to as a job description, can attract candidates to apply for the position (Richardson et al., 2016). Before posting an open principal position, district officials should be thoughtful about what is included in the job description so that they provide a rich portrayal of the position. Boilerplate job descriptions might be easy and cost efficient, but viewing this as an important aspect of the recruitment process will add to the quality and fit of potential applicants.

With technology advancements over the last two decades, school districts have been able to maintain their own robust websites that generally include a section for human resources. These websites allow for easily identifiable sections that post teacher, classified, and administrator job openings and provide a cost-effective way to advertise job openings. Through the use of social media, these postings can be disseminated widely and direct interested individuals to the district website for additional information.

Unfortunately, job postings on a district website leave school districts vulnerable to only those who monitor these websites. Well-qualified (and even interested) applicants could simply miss the posting. A critical part of recruitment is actively seeking individuals who possess the right qualifications to support the school and propel it forward. Since the traffic of school district websites tend to have localized followings of current parents and community members, school districts can also utilize professional association websites to post principal positions (Ohio Association of Secondary Schools, n.d.).

Unlike local district sites, state professional associations have a larger reach and have office personnel who can provide guidance to interested applicants due to their knowledge of statewide school administrators. Like district sites, these sites too are also limited to the individuals who monitor them regularly. Relying on job postings alone can perpetuate the gap between desirable districts and those who struggle to attract candidates (Pijanowski & Brady, 2009; Richardson et al., 2016; Stark-Price et al., 2006).

Attend Job Fairs and Partner With Local Universities

Job fairs also continue to be a common recruitment strategy in K–12 education (Odden, 2011). These are generally sponsored by local universities looking to assist their recent education graduates (i.e., teachers and principals) in finding employment in K–12 school districts. Unfortunately, job fairs continue to cater more to future teachers than school principals. To that end, state and national professional associations do include vendor fairs as part of their annual conferences, and school districts can purchase booths to promote their schools, advertise principal openings, and hold on-site interviews.

Job fairs are just one aspect of a partnership between universities and K–12 school districts. In addition to job fairs, it is important for K–12 districts to work closely with local universities to establish strong pipelines to leadership (Fuller et al., 2018; Fusarelli et al., 2018). K–12 districts are uniquely positioned to partner with local universities since they employ teachers interested in earning school leadership degrees.

District and building leaders can tap teachers with promising talent (Myung et al., 2011) as well as promote university programs that mirror their expectations for school leaders. Although not an active form of principal recruitment, partnerships between K–12 and local university school leadership programs can open up communication about future leaders worth consideration for principal openings.

Provide Incentives

For districts that struggle to attract qualified applicants, providing incentives as part of the job posting can catch the attention of otherwise uninterested individuals (Odden, 2011). Providing signing bonuses, covering moving expenses, providing tuition reimbursement, paying for continued education (e.g., a doctorate), or paying off existing student loans could prove attractive for principal candidates. More research needs to be done to better understand if providing such incentives actually makes a difference in the pool of qualified applicants for open principal positions.

Considering employee referrals, using technology to post jobs, attending job fairs and partnering with local universities, and using incentives are practical methods used in the recruitment of principals. These recruitment methods are utilized to secure candidates for open principal positions, especially depending on need. Wealthy suburban districts continue to have the largest applicant pools (Pijanowski & Brady, 2009; Winter & Morgenthal, 2002) and demonstrate less need to actively recruit. Posting the position is generally the only form of recruitment necessary to attract candidates.

Conversely, poor rural and large urban school districts continue to have the highest shortage of qualified principal candidates (Pijanowski & Brady, 2009; Whitaker, 2003) and need to actively recruit. Considering referrals, broadcasting openings widely, securing strong university partnerships, and offering incentives can work to broaden the pool of interested candidates. These trends continue to be perpetuated by school district reputations. Applicants gravitate toward schools and districts with the best reputations of student demographics and achievement (Loeb et al., 2010; Papa, 2007). This underscores the need to consider alternative recruitment strategies to hire for the role of the principalship.

ALTERNATIVE RECRUITMENT STRATEGIES

Although empirical research surrounding principal recruitment continues to be slim (Pounder & Young, 1996; Lee & Mao, 2020), attempts to secure principal candidates do take place through alternative recruitment methods (Lortie, 2009; Myung et al., 2011; Pounder et al., 2003). When school districts do not have formal recruitment practices in effect, these informal approaches provide them with more control over administering vacancies as they occur (Korach & Cosner, 2017). This section highlights some common approaches such as "grow your own" programs, assistant principal mentoring and professional development, and principal preparation programs.

"Grow Your Own" Programs

According to Joseph (2009), some districts have implemented "grow your own" leadership programs. These initiatives are becoming more popular as a cost-effective way for school districts to gain a level of control over filling open administrative positions. (Joseph, 2009; Miracle, 2006; Wood et al., 2013).

One of the most important things we can do for the educational leadership profession is encourage those with promise to become school leaders (Fusarelli et al., 2018). This is supported by Lortie's (2009) finding that almost three out of every four school principals had been mentored by another leader prior to entering administration. Often referred to as "tapping" (Myung el al., 2011), veteran school leaders can handpick from already existing teacher talent and prepare them with appropriate experiences to learn the role and demonstrate an ability to do the job prior to an actual opening.

Additionally, these sponsored mobility practices (Lortie, 2009) provide a window into potential areas of weakness that can be overcome by training and experience and avoid a steep learning curve upon being hired as a principal (Grunow et al., 2010; Korach & Cosner, 2017; Shumate et al., 2005). Educators themselves can also work to be seen by district officials by seeking out opportunities and offering to take on more leadership responsibilities around the school. This can be mutually beneficial by helping already busy leaders distribute some of the workload (Spillane et al., 2007) and also allowing future leadership candidates to demonstrate skill and fit for the principalship.

Although "grow your own" programs have positive aspects, a potential pitfall is maintaining an imbalance in the principalship regarding diversity (Loder, 2005). The majority of public school educators still identify as White (Will, 2020) and the percentage of Black school principals has not changed in over three decades (Hill et al., 2016). Whether out of necessity or because it is an easy way to grow talent within, if the principal pipeline is already predominately White, "grow your own" programs are inclined to perpetuate a field of White school leaders. It is important to also focus on active recruitment strategies that could attract persons of color into the principalship (Davis et al., 2017; Myung et al., 2011).

Additionally, these programs can also limit the growth of gender diversity in the profession. Although the number of female principals has grown (Fuller et al., 2018; Mertz, 2006), a continued equity gap limits the number of female administrators who will have mentors with similar lived experiences (Lee & Mao, 2020). However, "grow your own" programs, despite the potential for more of the same, generally can create effective pipelines for future principal openings (Fusarelli et al., 2018).

Assistant Principal Mentoring and Professional Development

In addition to "grow your own" programs, another alternative method for recruiting principal candidates is the development of assistant principals (Fusarelli et al., 2018; Goodlad, 2004). Except for small school districts, the assistant principal is an established role in K–12 schools and serves as an additional pipeline to the principalship.

Assistant principals are already hired leaders in a school district and have demonstrated an initial strength in skill and knowledge that aligned with the district's needs. Like the leadership pipeline of "grow your own" programs (Fuller, 2017; Korach & Cosner, 2017), a focus on assistant principal growth can prepare multiple individuals with the requisite skills to assume future head principal openings (Marshall & Hooley, 2006; Oliver, 2005).

Assistant principals can be grouped in leadership cohorts and learn advanced skills needed to be successful in future principal positions (Gurley et al., 2015; Odden, 2011). These cohorts are a cost-effective way for school districts to determine which aspects of the principalship they want covered in addition to providing individualized learning for assistant principals based on gaps in competencies (e.g., discipline scenarios) specific to building level (e.g., elementary, middle, high).

Additionally, this provides another window for viewing the skills and traits of individual assistant principals to see if they might be a good fit for principal openings in the future. This inserts a level of quality control over future hires (Joseph, 2009) that promotes both recruitment and succession interests for the school district.

Principal Preparation Programs

Levine (2005) argues that principal preparation programs do not offer relevant coursework or adequately expose future school leaders to the realities of the work. Further, additional studies have highlighted that the balance between theory and practice in principal preparation programs often tips in favor of more theoretical views (Bailey, 2014; Cosner et al., 2015; Gordon et al., 2016; Roegman & Woulfin, 2019). Although the intent here is not to engage in dialogue about what makes for a quality university principal preparation program, this does shed light on the importance of establishing partnerships between K–12 schools and universities—a strategy that can serve as an alternative recruitment method.

These two bodies, the school district and the university, should not exist in isolation from each other. In a sense, both need each other to survive and must remain in communication about needs, challenges, and desired outcomes for future school leaders. These partnerships allow K–12 school districts to articulate gaps they see in new principal hires and conversely position university preparation programs to promote the strengths of pre-service leaders based on a match between their individual strengths and K–12 school district needs.

CONCLUSION

Pounder and Young (1996) provided one of the first notable calls surrounding principals leaving the profession and an emerging need for principal recruitment. Whether focusing on student achievement (Hancock et al., 2006), stress and long hours (Pounder and Merrill 2001; Winter et al. 2002), or the concept of "graying" school administrators (Fusarelli et al., 2018), the need to tailor recruitment of principals is not new. Unfortunately, over two decades later research on principal recruitment remains scant (Cieminski, 2018; Lee & Mao, 2020).

Although more recent studies have focused on reasons why principal shortages might be occurring (Fusarelli et al., 2018; Lee & Mao, 2020), there is still little to no work that highlights actual methods of principal recruitment. To that end, we are left with blending both empirical research and common practitioner approaches that support the recruitment of future principals. Still today, traditional methods like employee referral, job postings, job fairs, and incentives are used to attract candidates. Alternative methods like "grow your own" programs, assistant principal learning academies, and K–12 school and university partnerships are also employed to recruit principal applicants.

All of this underscores the need for more empirical studies on existing strategies that actually work to attract principals to the profession. And why?

Because this is a critically important job. We know that teachers have long showed a desire to enter the principalship and want to make a greater difference (Parylo et al., 2012; Pounder & Merrill, 2001). As well, veteran principals state they would do it all over again if they could (Pijanowski et al., 2009). This shows great promise in that there continues to be an interest in the important work of the principalship, and it is our charge to better understand how to effectively recruit the best and brightest into this position.

REFERENCES

Agosto, V., & Roland, E. (2018). Intersectionality and educational leadership: A critical review. *Review of Research in Education, 42*(1), 255–285.

Bailey, S. (2014). Scholar-practitioner leadership: A conceptual foundation. *International Journal of Progressive Education, 10*(3), 48–59.

Castetter, W. B., & Young, I. P. (2003). *The human resource function in educational administration.* Merrill.

Chion Kenney, L. (2003). Confidential searches. *School Administrator, 60*(6), 6–12.

Cieminski, A. B. (2018). Practices that support leadership succession and principal retention. *Education Leadership Review, 19*(1), 21–41.

Collins, J. (2001). *Good to great: Why some companies make the leap . . . and others don't.* Harper Business.

Cosner, S., Tozer, S., Zavitkovsky, P., & Whalen, S. P. (2015). Cultivating exemplary school leadership preparation at a research intensive university. *Journal of Research on Leadership Education, 10*(1), 11–38.

Creswell, J. W. (2014). *Research design: Qualitative, quantitative, and mixed methods approaches.* SAGE Publications.

Davis, B. W., Gooden, M. A., & Bowers, A. J. (2017). Pathways to the principalship: An event history analysis of the careers of teachers with principal certification. *American Educational Research Journal, 54*(2), 207–240

Davis, S. H. (2005). *School leadership study: Developing successful principals.* Stanford Educational Leadership Institute.

Fuller, E. J., Pendola, A., & LeMay, M. (2018). Who should be our leader? Examining female representation in the principalship across geographic locales in Texas public schools. *Journal of Research in Rural Education, 34*(4), 1–21.

Fusarelli, B. C., Fusarelli, L. D., & Riddick, F. (2018). Planning for the future: Leadership development and succession planning in education. *Journal of Research on Leadership Education, 13*(3), 286–313.

Gajda, R., & Militello, M. (2008). Recruiting and retaining school principals: What we can learn from practicing administrators. *AASA Journal of Scholarship and Practice, 5*(1), 14–20.

Goodlad, J. (2004). *A place called school.* McGraw-Hill.

Gordon, S. P., Oliver, J., & Solis, R. (2016). Successful innovations in educational leadership preparation. *International Journal of Educational Leadership Preparation, 11*(2), 51–70.

Grissom, J. A., Mitani, H., & Woo, D. S. (2019). Principal preparation programs and principal outcomes. *Educational Administration Quarterly, 55*(1), 73–115.

Grissom, J. A., Rodriguez, L. A., & Kern, E. C. (2017). Teacher and principal diversity and the representation of students of color in gifted programs: Evidence from national data. *The Elementary School Journal, 117*(3), 396–422.

Grunow, A., Horng, E. H., & Loeb, S. (2010). *Succession management in schools* [Working paper]. Stanford University, Center for Education Policy Analysis.

Gurley, D. K., Anast-May, L., & Lee, H. T. (2015). Developing instructional leaders through assistant principals' academy: A partnership for success. *Education and Urban Society, 47*(2), 207–241.

Hancock, D. R., Black, T., & Bird, J. J. (2006). A study of factors that influence teachers to become school administrators. *Journal of Educational Research, 6*(1), 91–105.

Hargreaves, A. (2009). Leadership succession and sustainable improvement. *School Administrator, 66*(11), 10–14.

Hargreaves, A., & Fink, D. (2006). *Sustainable leadership*. Jossey-Bass.

Hill, J., Ottem, R., & DeRoche, J. (2016). *Trends in public and private school principal demographics and qualifications: 1987–88 to 2011–12*. (Report No. 2016-189). National Center for Education Statistics, U.S. Department of Education.

Joseph, S. (2009). Planning to grow your own principal preparation programs: Cultivating excellence in tough economic times. *Educational Planning, 18*(2), 35–41.

Kamler, E. (2009). Decade of difference (1995–2005): An examination of the superintendent search consultants' process on Long Island. *Educational Administration Quarterly, 45*(1), 115–144.

Kearney, K. (2010). *Effective principals for California schools: Building a coherent leadership development system*. WestEd. https://www.wested.org/resources/effective-principals-for-california-schools-building-a-coherent-leadership-development-system/#

Korach, S., & Cosner, S. (2017). Developing the leadership pipeline: Comprehensive leadership development. In M. Young & G. Crow (Eds.), *Handbook of research on the education of school leaders* (pp. 262–282). Routledge.

Lawler, E. E., & Boudreau, J. W. (2009). *Achieving excellence in human resource management*. Stanford University Press.

Lee, S. W., & Mao, X. (2020). Recruitment and selection of principals: A systematic review. *Educational Management Administration & Leadership, 51*(1), 1–24. https://doi.org/10.1177/1741143220969694

Levine, A. (2005). *Educating school leaders*. The Education Schools Project. https://eric.ed.gov/?id=ED504142

Loder, T. L. (2005). On deferred dreams, callings, and revolving doors of opportunity: African American women's reflections on becoming principals. *Urban Review, 37*(3), 243–265.

Loeb, S., Kalogrides, D., & Horng, E. L. (2010). Principal preferences and the uneven distribution of principals across schools. *Educational Evaluation and Policy Analysis, 32*(2), 205–229.

Lortie, D. (2009). *School principal: Managing in public.* University of Chicago Press.

Marshall, C., & Hooley, R. M. (2006). *The assistant principal: Leadership choices and challenges.* Corwin Press.

McCarthy, M. (2015). Reflections on the evolution of educational leadership preparation programs in the United States and challenges ahead. *Journal of Educational Administration, 53*(3), 416–438.

McDonnell, L. M. (2012). Educational accountability and policy feedback. *Educational Policy, 27*(2), 170–189.

Merriam-Webster. (n.d.). Recruitment. In *Merriam-Webster.com dictionary.* https://www.merriam-webster.com/dictionary/recruitment

Mertz, N. T. (2006). The promise of Title IX: Longitudinal study of gender in urban school administration, 1972 to 2002. *Urban Education, 41*(6), 544–559.

Miracle, T. L. (2006). *An analysis of a district-level aspiring principals training program.* Dissertation Abstracts International (UMI No. 3228666).

Myung, J., Loeb, S., & Horng, E. (2011). Tapping the principal pipeline: Identifying talent for future school leadership in the absence of formal succession management programs. *Educational Administration Quarterly, 47*(5), 695–727.

National Association of Secondary School Principals. (1998). *Salaries paid principals and assistant principals.* Educational Research Service.

Odden, A. R. (2011). *Strategic management of human capital in education: Improving instructional practice and student learning in schools.* Routledge.

Ohio Association of Secondary School Administrators (n.d.). *Job posting board.* https://oassa.org/jobs/

Oliver, R. (2005). Assistant principal professional growth and development: A matter that cannot be left to chance. *Educational Leadership and Administration, 17,* 89–100.

Papa, F. (2007). Why do principals change schools? A multivariate analysis of principal retention. *Leadership and Policy in Schools, 6*(3), 267–290.

Parylo, O., Zepeda, S. J., & Bengtson, E. (2012). Career paths in educational leadership: examining principals' narratives. *Alberta Journal of Educational Research, 58*(4), 565–599.

Pijanowski, J. C., & Brady, K. P. (2009). The influence of salary in attracting and retaining school leaders. *Education and Urban Society, 42*(1), 25–41.

Pijanowski, J. C., Hewitt, P. M., & Brady, K. P. (2009). Superintendents' perceptions of the principal shortage. *NASSP Bulletin, 93*(2), 85–95.

Pounder, D. G., & Merrill, R. J. (2001). Job desirability of the high school principalship: A job choice theory perspective. *Educational Administration Quarterly, 37*(1), 27–57.

Pounder, D. G., & Young, I. P. (1996). Recruitment and selection of educational administrators: Priorities for today's schools. In K. Leithwood (Ed.) & A.W. Hart (Section Ed.), *The International Handbook of Educational Leadership* (pp. 279–308). Springer.

Pounder, D. G., Galvin, P., & Shepherd, P. (2003). An analysis of the United States educational administrator shortage. *Australian Journal of Education, 47*, 133–146.

Richardson, J. W., Watts, D. S., Hollis, E., & McLeod, S. (2016). Are changing school needs reflected in principal job ads? *NASSP Bulletin, 100*(1), 71–92.

Roegman, R., & Woulfin, S. (2019). Got theory? Reconceptualizing the nature of the theory-practice gap in K–12 educational leadership. *Journal of Educational Administration, 57*(1), 2–20.

Rothwell, W. J. (2010). *Effective succession planning: Ensuring leadership continuity and building talent from* within (4th ed.). AMACOM.

Roza, M. (2003). *A matter of definition: Is there truly a shortage of school principals?* Center on Reinventing Public Education, University of Washington. https://www.wallacefoundation.org/knowledge-center/Documents/Is-There-Truly-a-Shortage-of-School-Principals.pdf

Seashore Louis, K., Leithwood, K., Wahlstrom, K. L., & Anderson, S. E. (2010). *Investigating the links to improved student learning: Final report of research findings*. Learning from Leadership Project, The Wallace Foundation. https://www.wallacefoundation.org/knowledge-center/Documents/Investigating-the-Links-to-Improved-Student-Learning-Executive-Summary.pdf

Shumate, B. T., Muñoz, M. A., & Winter, P. A. (2005). Evaluating teacher-leaders for careers as administrators: Effects of job attributes, teacher leader role, and teaching assignment area. *Journal of Personnel Evaluation in Education, 18*, 21–38.

Snodgrass Rangel, V. (2018). A review of the literature on principal turnover. *Review of Educational Research, 88*(1), 87–124.

Somekh, B., & Lewin, C. (2005). *Research methods in the social sciences*. SAGE Publications.

Spillane, J. P., Camburn, E., & Pareja, A. (2007). Taking a distributed perspective to the school principal's workday. *Leadership and Policy in Schools, 6*(1), 103–125.

Stark-Price, G. A., Munoz, M. A., Winter, P. A., & Petrosko, J. M. (2006). Recruiting principals to lead low-performing schools: Effects on job attractiveness. *The Journal of Personnel Evaluation in Education, 19*, 69–83.

Thornton, M. E., Barakat, M., Grooms, A. A., Locke, L. A., & Reyes-Guerra, D. (2022). Revolutionary perspectives for leadership preparation: A case of a networked improvement community. *Journal of Research on Leadership Education, 17*(1), 90–108.

Tomal, D. R., & Schilling, C. A. (2018). *Human resource management: Optimizing organizational performance* (2nd ed.). Rowman & Littlefield.

Whitaker, K. S. (2003). Principal role changes and influence on principal recruitment and selection: An international perspective. *Journal of Educational Administration, 41*(1) 37–54.

Will, M. (2020, April 14). *Still mostly White and female: New federal data on the teaching profession*. Education Week. https://www.edweek.org/leadership/still-mostly-white-and-female-new-federal-data-on-the-teaching-profession/2020/04

Winter, P. A., & Morgenthal, J. R. (2002). Principal recruitment in a reform environment: Effects of school achievement and school level on applicant attraction to the job. *Educational Administration Quarterly, 38*(3), 319–340.

Winter, P. A., Rinehart, J. S., & Munoz, M. A. (2002). Principal recruitment: An empirical evaluation of a school district's internal pool of principal certified personnel. *Journal of Personnel Evaluation in Education, 16*(2), 129–141.

Wood, J. N., Finch, K., & Mirecki, R. M. (2013). If we get you, how can we keep you? Problems with recruiting and retaining rural administrators. *Rural Educator, 34*(2), 1–13.

Zepeda, S. J., Bengston, E., & Parylo, O. (2012). Examining the planning and management of principal succession. *Journal of Educational Administration, 50*(2), 136–158.

Chapter 2

Principal Recruitment in New Zealand

The Role of Boards of Trustees

Gülay Erin Dalgıç, University of Auckland

Effective and powerful educational leadership is critical for quality teaching and student achievement (Leithwood et al., 2004; Robinson et al., 2009). Investing in developing, appointing and retaining effective principals is a cost-effective way to improve the quality of education (Service et al., 2016). However, higher expectations placed on school principals globally have turned the principalship into a much more complex and demanding role than ever before. Resulting changes in the roles of principals have caused an increase in turnover rates by making the role less attractive.

Additionally, with the high number of principals reaching retirement age (Robertson, 2011), it has become necessary for governments and local governing bodies to improve principal development, appointment, and retention policies and practices (OECD, 2008; Service et al., 2016). The governance framework that operates in New Zealand (NZ) schools also contributes to the complexities of the role, by making principals chief advisors to the Board of Trustees (BOT) (Wylie, 2009). The BOT plays a pivotal role in the governance of schools in New Zealand.

Following the 1989 education reforms, the BOT gained unregulated power to recruit the principal of their choice, unlike in any other education system with self-managed schools (Wylie, 2002). The BOT's role in the governance of schools in New Zealand includes its processes and structures to ensure accountability, transparency, responsiveness, stability, equity, and inclusiveness.

This chapter will explore the Board of Trustees' practices and challenges associated with principal recruitment and appointment in NZ schools. The chapter first describes the school governance and the BOT's role in NZ primary and secondary schools. It will then explore the challenges of the BOT's principal appointment approaches and practices that contribute to existing inequities in education. The final section explores the initiatives taken by the government and support mechanisms provided to the BOT in principal appointment processes. At the end of the chapter, the reader will be provided with recommendations for improving the BOT principal appointment processes.

BACKGROUND

Social equity and economic stability have always been the main drivers shaping NZ's educational system, aligned with the country's social, political, and economic context. In the 1980s, the NZ government started a reform movement due to a need for economic stability and the inability of the country to compete in the global market. This reform movement focused on the educational system to provide long-term economic stability in the country. Therefore, the Task Force to Review Educational Administration was established in 1987 to review the schooling system. The results of this review showed that

- administrative capabilities were not responsive to new technologies;
- the values and demographics of the society were changing;
- management systems were not supporting efficient and effective processes; and
- the number of decision points between the center and schools was not helping these processes (Novlan, 1998).

In response to the results of the 1987 review, the educational system was decentralized with the Education Act of 1989 and Tomorrow's Schools Reform. Under the new scheme, the school and its community gained financial autonomy and control over local school policy. The government kept its control over policymaking at the national level, assessing students, schools, and charter requirements. This resulted in enormous downsizing in the Head Office of Education, and the district boards of trustees were dismantled. The main changes to school governance after the 1987 review were the following:

- The principals and Board of Trustees to share the entire governance and management of schools. The new scheme saw the BOT become the

principal's and teachers' legal employer, with control over appointment, performance management, and professional development responsibilities (Anderson, 2009).
- The school charter was put into practice. A charter is a key planning document that outlines the school's strategic plan, learning programs, and activities to meet local needs aligned with national guidelines. The charter is a yearly plan to be sent and approved by the Ministry of Education (MoE) (Novlan, 1998).
- The Educational Review Office (ERO) was established as an independent government organization to assess the schools based on meeting their charter objectives (Novlan, 1998).

The reforms changed the roles of principals and increased their workloads by adding more administrative responsibilities and assigning them the role of chief advisor to the board, on top of other professional leadership responsibilities (Wylie, 2009). The decentralization process forced principals to spend more time supporting the BOT, building maintenance, strategic planning, marketing, public relations, and community sponsorship (Wylie & MacDonald, 2020).

Since the responsibility of appointing and employing principals was given to the BOT, boards have struggled to attain the necessary number of applications for advertised principal positions, ensure the quality of the applicants, and run a reliable and effective selection process (Wylie, 2002; Tomorrow's Schools Independent Taskforce, 2018).

BOARDS OF TRUSTEES (BOT) AND ISSUES WITH THEIR FUNCTIONING

In New Zealand, every school is governed by a voluntary school board called the Board of Trustees, which is comprised of the principal, three to seven parent-elected trustees, and a trustee elected by school staff. A student trustee elected by the students is added to the board at the secondary school level (Anderson, 2009). The Education Act of 1989 provides the board with the flexibility to determine its total size. This flexibility enables the board to recruit parent representatives with the wide-ranging abilities and expertise required for effective school governance.

The ERO (2014) describes the aspects of effective school governance and legal functions of the boards as

- providing vision, values, and strategic direction;

- ensuring a quality relationship between governance, leadership, and management roles;
- addressing student achievement, including the alignment of resources, policies, and practices;
- ensuring effective allocation of human, financial, and property resources; and
- providing evidence for strategic planning and self-review.

Principal appointment constitutes only one part of the human resources allocation role of the BOT.

Boards are expected to have a balance of specific skills and attributes to ensure that their varying responsibilities are being met. One problem with the selection of board members is that there are no set standards for becoming a board member. Any parents or caregivers of students and people from the wider community can run for board membership if they "have a commitment to the education of children and a desire to improve student achievement" (Ministry of Education, n.d., *Your school board*).

Board members can receive free advice and support from the New Zealand School Trustees Association (NZSTA, 2008) after becoming a part of the board. The NZSTA also provides professional development opportunities for members. However, none of these is compulsory. There is no assessment of the skills and backgrounds of the board members when they join the board. It is up to the board member to decide what support and capabilities they need to acquire to carry out the roles of the BOT.

Another problem associated with decentralized school governance, which resonates with the international literature, is the level of involvement expected from the volunteer board members, namely parents. The positions in the BOT require a high level of involvement. Research shows a correlation between school size, location, income decile level, and BOT members' involvement (Anderson, 2009).

The willingness of the BOT to be actively involved in the requirements of its roles and the high turnover rate within the BOT are issues, especially in small, low decile and rural schools. Additionally, there is more reluctance by the board members to participate in board meetings and to take on board responsibilities in those schools (Anderson, 2009).

One other possible issue between principals and their boards is how they maintain their relationships. *Positive relationships between principals and their boards* are based on trust, openness, transparency, and clarity around roles and responsibilities (Leggett et al., 2016). The BOT's role as the principal's and the teachers' legal employer can create unequal power dynamics and inconsistency of standards across schools over time (Anderson, 2009).

However, studies show that most principals are in positive relationships with their boards and believe their boards add value to their schools (Anderson, 2009; Wylie & MacDonald, 2020). In a survey representing 32% of school principals in New Zealand, only a small percentage (8–9%) of principals expressed experiencing stress in the relationship (Anderson, 2009).

In cases where there is a board-principal conflict, the principals could refer to several sources of advice to solve the conflict. The New Zealand School Trustees Association (NZSTA, 2008), unions, MoE, and principal organizations can be listed as the critical support sources in cases of a board-principal conflict. However, research shows that the principals feel isolation and extreme stress in serious conflict situations with their boards when they cannot get the support they need from these key organizations (Anderson, 2009).

In cases of conflict, the existing support mechanisms work better for boards than for principals. In serious employment disputes with their boards, principals do not expect support from the NZSTA, as it represents the school board, and principals' associations do not provide financial support to the principal to take legal action. Further, there is no known research that demonstrates the relationship between principal-board conflicts and the variation of schools (size, location, decile) in the system.

Boards have an indirect positive impact on the professional development of their principals by providing them with opportunities for group reflection through board meetings and self-reflection in preparing reports and reviews for their boards (Dalgıç & Bakioğlu, 2014). Boards are responsible for providing professional development opportunities for their principals.

Research also shows disparities among boards regarding how they fulfill their responsibility to provide professional development for their principal and teachers. Boards provide the principal with more professional challenge and stimulation in larger schools than in small, low decile and rural schools (Anderson, 2009).

PROBLEMS WITH THE BOT PRINCIPAL APPOINTMENTS

Recruiting and appointing principals are among the most challenging tasks of the boards. The success of the process relies on obtaining robust applications and running a well-structured, well-informed, and fair selection process (Robertson, 2011). BOTs show disparities in their principal appointment processes as they lack the skills and experience to carry out their employer roles (Brooking, 2005, 2007; Macpherson, 2009).

Gender Bias

Gender imbalance has always been significant in the NZ teacher workforce. The number of female teachers comprised 73 to 76% of the whole primary and secondary teacher workforce in the last twenty years (MoE, n.d., *Teacher numbers*). However, the dominance of female teachers is not observed in principalship positions.

At the beginning of the 2000s, the chance of a male teacher becoming a principal was six times higher than that of a female teacher (Brooking, 2005). Although the number of female principals increased from 42 to 54% in the last twenty years, this increase is not proportionate to the number of female teachers and senior female leaders in the teacher workforce (see Figure 2.1).

International research indicates the barriers to women attaining principal positions as (a) framing the principal role as masculine (Coleman, 2005), (b) cultural motives and stereotypes (Oplatka & Tamir, 2009), (c) lack of mentorship and role models (Jean-Marie, 2013), (d) gendered family responsibilities (Wylie et al., 2020), and (e) women underestimating their leadership skills (Roach et al., 2017). Parallel to the literature on barriers to women attaining principal positions, in New Zealand, we see the tendency of BOTs to appoint men to principal roles, owing to the factors explained above (Brooking, 2005; Wylie et al., 2020).

Brooking (2005, 2008) and Brooking et al.'s (2003) research on principal appointment approaches of board chairs, principals, and board advisors shows inconsistency in following the legislation and more instinctive than well-informed decision-making processes. To illustrate this, while 80% of

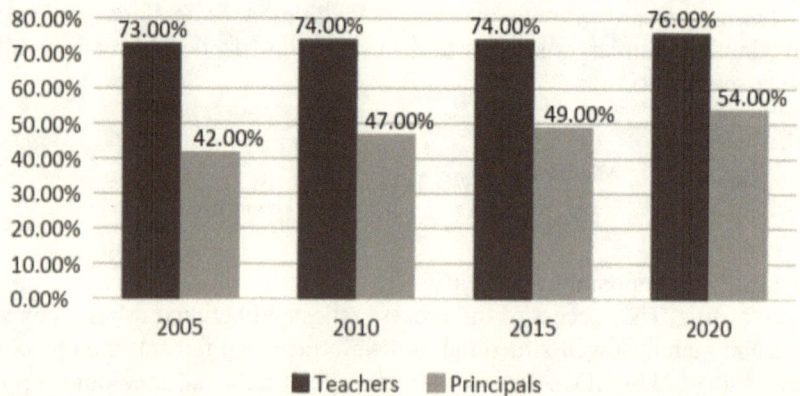

Figure 2.1. Female Representation in the Teacher and Principal Workforce, 2005–2020. *Teacher Headcount: Time Series Data. Retrieved March 15, 2022, from https://www.educationcounts.govt.nz/statistics/teacher-numbers#3. Copyright 2022 by Ministry of Education.*

the senior leadership positions were comprised of women, 60% of primary school principal appointments were made from the pool of male teachers, which constituted 18% of the whole primary teacher population in 2002 (Brooking, 2005).

In addition, Robertson's (2011) more recent study shows that while women made up 53% of the shortlisted applicants in 2009–2010 principal appointments, they only represented 44% of those appointed. This indicates some improvement in women's principal appointments, although not enough to achieve equitable access to and representation in principal positions.

Some of the main justifications made by BOTs for appointing men over women in principal positions are biases regarding the masculinist connotations of leadership associated with discipline and authority: Men are seen as role models for boys, leading sports and education outside classroom activities (Brooking, 2005, 2008; Brooking et al. 2003).

Although there are concerns about the functionality of the school boards, particularly in principal recruitment, there are also many good examples of BOT practices that bring innovative and flexible solutions to the challenges of principal appointment. One of the earliest good examples of the innovative thinking of the BOT dates back to the 1990s (the Selwyn College co-principalship model).

Selwyn College is a high school in Auckland, and, when the principal position was advertised, the school was already being successfully led by the two deputy principals (a woman and a man) because of the ongoing health issues of the principal. However, owing to the demanding and complex responsibilities of the principalship, none of the deputy principals were keen to apply for the job.

Carefully scrutinizing the regulations, a BOT member who was a lawyer found a legal way to enable a co-principal model (Glenny et al., 1996), which worked effectively for many years. Since then, this case has worked as an exemplar for creating other co-principalship roles in NZ schools.

BOTS LACK THE REQUIRED SKILLS FOR RECRUITMENT AND SUPERVISORY ROLES

An ongoing issue for the BOTs is a lack of experience necessary to effectively fulfill their governance roles (Robinson et al., 2003). The results of the 2019 national survey for school boards reveal that 86% of trustees had not served on a school board before. For 49%, the BOT was their first governance experience (Wylie & MacDonald, 2020).

Studies show an association between school size, location, decile ranking, ethnic makeup, and the skills and expertise of the BOT (Brooking, 2005;

Morrison, 2013; NZSTA, 2008; Stevens & Wylie, 2017; Youngs, 2005). The 2013 national survey revealed that boards of low decile schools identified a need for skill development in areas like strategic planning and finance, employer role, building links with local *iwi* (which can be translated in English as *tribe*, the largest political grouping in Māori society that takes its name from a founding ancestor), and developing Pasifika networks and leadership (Stevens & Wylie, 2017).

In contrast, large urban schools are more likely to have high-status business executives on their boards (Brooking, 2005). Aligned with these research findings, Youngs's (2005) study points out that small and rural school boards must identify needs for leadership development.

A 2006 survey conducted by the New Zealand Council for Educational Research (NZCER) also identified that principals of low decile schools rate the experience and skills of their BOTs lower than do principals of high decile schools (Wylie, 2007). These research findings reveal an alarming situation regarding existing societal inequities and the ways in which school boards may contribute to these inequities.

SUPPORT PROVIDED TO BOTS FOR PRINCIPAL APPOINTMENT

The government has established various support mechanisms and initiatives to aid the BOT in its principal appointment process. The board is mainly guided by the regulations and guidelines agreed to by the MoE and NZSTA. There are also principal professional organizations, unions, NZSTA helpline services, and the Ministry's School Support Services division to support the BOT and provide advisory services.

Unlike in other countries, in NZ's school governance system, the BOT is not obliged to consult with other authorities regarding employment-related responsibilities (Anderson, 2009). However, almost all boards believe in the usefulness of getting advice in the principal appointment process, and nearly all (98%) use additional expertise in the appointment process.

Private consultants, current principals, other local schools' BOTs and school support services are some of the most widely accessed support sources, followed by support from the MoE and a recruitment agency (Robertson, 2011). The BOT generally refers to their local MoE advisor to get recommendations for private consultants.

Some also approach other school boards in their community that recently appointed a principal to get advice on how to plan the principal appointment process and from whom to get support (K. Anderson, personal communication, May 13, 2022). Although BOTs involve other parties in different stages of the principal appointment process, the BOT is the sole decision-maker of the appointment process, which makes it accountable for the outcome of the process.

In recruiting principals, boards seek advice in (a) developing the job description and specifications, (b) the advertising processes to attract suitable candidates, (c) short-listing candidates, (d) having someone with additional expertise as a member of the interview panel, and (e) the practicalities and legalities of making an appointment in the final choice between candidates (Robertson, 2011). Boards also use email surveys to consult with their community in the recruitment process for a new principal. Parents are asked about desired attributes and key skills in anonymous surveys to help inform the new principal selection.

However, studies have identified significant differences between the school types, decile and location, and the BOT's need and tendency to access support in the principal appointment process. One interesting finding that highlights the socioeconomic disparities across schools and their boards is found in Morrison's (2013) research.

In her research on board chairs' experiences of principal appointment, Morrison (2013) interviewed four board chairs of schools from different socioeconomic areas. The study revealed that board chairs of schools in high socioeconomic areas show greater awareness, knowledge, and effective use of existing supports provided to the BOT.

GOVERNMENT INITIATIVES TO IMPROVE PRINCIPAL APPOINTMENT

The support mechanisms provided to school boards for principal appointments have not brought a sustainable solution to principal shortages and appointment issues in urban, small, and full primary schools that cover years (grades) 0–8. While some schools attract many applicants for the principal position, others obtain one or none (Robertson, 2011). As part of the Investing in Educational Success (IES) initiative, the government established two schemes, with a vision to help raise the learning and achievement of all children. The new schemes also aimed to provide more centralized and accountable support to BOTs in their employer role.

Principal Recruitment Allowance (PRA) was passed as part of IES to help BOTs obtain high-quality applicants for their principal vacancy advertisements. The scheme aims to attract principals who will ensure highly effective management and instructional leadership in schools with significant challenges to the student educational performance, student welfare, or the school's operation. Eligible principals are paid an allowance of $50,000 per year for a fixed period of three years, which may be paid for a maximum of two further fixed periods.

An evaluation of the PRA showed that with the implementation of the scheme, schools have been more able to attract highly effective principals, and principals describe the scheme as an "enabler" (MacDonald & Stevens, 2018). This practice resonates with turnaround principals or turnaround leadership, terms which have been widely used in the literature in the last two decades to describe the principals who improve their poorly achieving schools by transforming them (Fullan, 2006).

Communities of Learning (Kāhui Ako) is the other government scheme passed within the IES initiative to "improve equity and excellence by encouraging school, teacher, and community collaboration" by grouping schools into clusters (NANP, 2022). Communities of Learning enables schoolteachers, principals, and boards to collaborate and share ideas, learn from each other's experiences, and reflect and work together to reach a shared vision.

The scheme provides the boards a deeper understanding of the schools' communities and of changes and movements occurring across schools. Communities of Learning aims to make it easier for the school leaders and BOTs to support each other through improved school communication (NANP, 2022).

RECOMMENDATIONS

Based on the literature review in this chapter on principal appointment policy and practices in New Zealand, there are a few recommendations to improve the BOT principal appointment processes.

- It is important to ensure that attracting qualified candidates for the principalship is not the exclusive duty of the BOT. Currently, the only formal requirement to apply for the principalship is to be a registered teacher, although boards may specify their additional requirements. The government should ensure principal candidates' high quality with some structural changes in principalship eligibility criteria, like specifying additional formal requirements for the job.
- Members of school boards need to have competencies to interpret and develop policy and strategic plan documents. There should be a thorough assessment of the qualifications and backgrounds of each board member when they join the board, and they should be obliged to complete the training they are provided within their need areas.
- Rural, urban, low decile, small or large, and ethnically diverse schools face unique challenges. For example, rural schools encounter challenges

associated with isolation, inexperienced principals, or inadequate national funding. Therefore, targeted training is needed to meet the professional development needs of the BOTs in small, rural, and low decile schools.
- BOTs creating more flexible principal roles (such as co-principalships) should be encouraged to make the role more attractive to positively impact turnover rates.
- Government and school boards should ensure effective, unbiased principal appointment processes for all, particularly women. The government must introduce compulsory training for boards to fulfill their employer role. The appointment process should be transparent, accountable, and reported in detail to the MoE.
- The socioeconomic status of a school should not be a determinant of the board's composition and board members' skill sets. Although the government provides flexibility in the size of boards to ensure diversity and highly skilled board members, the current practice of board composition appears to foster already existing inequities in society.

- Accordingly, the government should fund the employment of qualified advisors on the boards of urban, low decile, and small schools. It should be mandatory for the BOT to have a leadership advisor on the board appointed by consensus to ensure a fair and accountable principal appointment process.

CONCLUSION

This chapter sought to identify challenges encountered by BOTs in principal appointment processes. Recruiting and appointing school principals is one of the BOT's most challenging governance roles because of the skills and expertise it requires. The composition of the BOT and its willingness to participate in board activities reveal disparities among schools. In small, low decile, and rural schools, it is more challenging to attract quality candidates and appoint the best suitable principal candidate.

Efforts to support BOTs in the principal appointment process through training, resources, and providing advisors are crucial but not enough to address the various challenges and limitations faced by boards. The BOT principal appointment process functions at the risk of reinforcing existing disparities and inequities in the education system.

The inability of BOTs to engender meaningful change in their own structure, function, and composition, as well as the socioeconomic and gender disparities across schools and their boards, reveals an urgent need for a central governing body to provide schools in need with support to ensure the composition of effective and high-quality BOTs. It is also crucial to ensure accountability in the principal appointment process. A leadership advisor for schools would help ensure that each BOT is equipped with the required capabilities: to establish guidelines, develop leadership capabilities in schools, and work with the advisor in appointing their principal.

REFERENCES

Anderson, C. (2009). *The New Zealand principals' experience of the school board as an employer: Survey report to the New Zealand Principals' Federation and the New Zealand Secondary Principals' Council*. New Zealand Principals' Federation. https://www.ppta.org.nz/publication-library/document/328

Brooking, K. (2005). Boards of trustees' selection of primary school principals in New Zealand. *Delta, 57*(1&2), 117–140.

Brooking, K. (2007). *Summary of the New Zealand literature on recruitment and retention of leaders: Issues, challenges, trends, and strategies for succession planning*. New Zealand Council for Educational Research.

Brooking, K. (2008). Future challenge of principal succession in New Zealand primary schools: Implications of quality and gender. *International Studies in Educational Administration, 36*(1), 41–55.

Brooking, K., Collins, G., Court, M., & O'Neill, J. (2003). Getting below the surface of the principal recruitment "crisis" in New Zealand primary schools. *Australian Journal of Education, 47*(2), 146–158.

Coleman, M. (2005). Gender and secondary school leadership. *International Studies in Educational Administration, 33*(2), 3–20.

Dalgıç, G., & Bakioğlu, A. (2014). The effect of stakeholders on the reflective practice of school principals: Practices in Istanbul and Copenhagen. *Teachers and Teaching, 20*(3), 289–313. https://doi.org/10.1080/13540602.2013.848524

Education Review Office (ERO). (2014). *School leadership that works*. https://ero.govt.nz/sites/default/files/2021-05/School-Leadership-that-Works-Nov-2016.pdf

Fullan, M. (2006). *Turnaround leadership*. Jossey-Bass.

Glenny, M., Lewis, D., & White, C. (1996). Power sharing at Selwyn College—Auckland, New Zealand: The co-principalship model. *Management in Education, 10*(4), 32–33.

Jean-Marie, G. (2013). The subtlety of age, gender, and race barriers: A case study of early-career African American female principals. *Journal of School Leadership, 23*(4), 615–639.

Leggett, B., Campbell-Evans, G., & Gray, J. (2016). Issues and challenges of school governance. *Leading & Managing, 2*(1), 36–56.

Leithwood, K., Seashore Louis, K., Anderson, S., & Wahlstrom, K. (2004). *How leadership influences student learning: A review of research for the Learning From

Leadership project. The Wallace Foundation. https://www.wallacefoundation.org/knowledge-center/Documents/How-Leadership-Influences-Student-Learning.pdf

MacDonald, J., & Stevens, E. (2018). *Formative evaluation of the principal recruitment allowance*. New Zealand Council for Educational Research. https://www.educationcounts.govt.nz/publications/schooling/formative-evaluation-of-the-principal-recruitment-allowance

Macpherson, R. (2009). How secondary principals view New Zealand's leadership preparation and succession strategies: Systematic professionalism or amateurism through serial incompetence? *Leading and Managing, 15*(2), 44–58.

Ministry of Education (MoE). (n.d.). *Teacher numbers*. https://www.educationcounts.govt.nz/statistics/teacher-numbers#3

Ministry of Education (MoE). (n.d.). *Your school board*. https://parents.education.govt.nz/primary-school/getting-involved-in-your-childs-school/your-school-board/#whatskills

Morrison, M. (2013). Parents appointing the principal: The experiences of four New Zealand primary school boards of trustees. *International Studies in Educational Administration, 41*(3), 29–44.

New Appointments National Panel (NANP). (2022). *Accomplishments, challenges, and reflections: The voices of Kāhui Ako practitioners*. https://www.ppta.org.nz/publication-library/document/1639

New Zealand School Trustees Association. (2008). *School governance: Board of trustees stocktake*. https://nzsta.org.nz/assets/Governance/Stocktake-Report-Findings-2008.pdf

Novlan, J. F. (1998). New Zealand's past and tomorrow's schools: Reasons, reforms and results. *School Leadership & Management, 18*(1), 7–18.

Oplatka, I., & Tamir, V. (2009). "I don't want to be a school head": Women deputy heads' insightful constructions of career advancement and retention. *Educational Management Administration & Leadership, 37*(2), 216–238.

Organisation for Economic Co-operation and Development (OECD). (2008). *School boards—school councils: Pointers for policy development*. Directorate for Education, Education and Training Policy Division. https://www.oecd.org/education/school/45162909.pdf

Roach, V., Tekleselassie, A., & Dalgic, G. (2017). *Understanding concepts of female educational leadership through self-in-relation data: A four-country analysis* [Conference session]. 2017 AERA Annual Meeting "Knowledge to Action: Achieving the Promise of Equal Educational Opportunity," San Antonio, TX.

Robertson, S. (2011). *Principal vacancies and appointments 2009–2010*. New Zealand Council for Educational Research. https://www.nzcer.org.nz/research/publications/principal-vacancies-and-appointments-2009-10

Robinson, V., Hohepa, M., & Lloyd, C. (2009). *School leadership and student outcomes: Identifying what works and why, Best Evidence Synthesis iteration (BES)*. Ministry of Education.

Robinson, V., Ward, L., & Timperley, H. (2003). Difficulties of governance: A layperson's job? *Educational Management & Administration, 31*(3): 263–281.

Service, B., Dalgıç, G. E., & Thornton, K. (2016). Implications of a shadowing/mentoring programme for aspiring principals. *International Journal of Mentoring and Coaching in Education, 5*(3), 253–271.

Stevens, E., & Wylie, C. (2017). *The work of school boards—trustees' perspectives: Findings from the NZCER national survey of primary and intermediate schools 2016*. New Zealand Council for Educational Research. https://www.nzcer.org.nz/research/publications/national-survey-trustees-perspectives

Tomorrow's Schools Independent Taskforce. (2018). *Our schooling futures: Stronger together*. Whiria Ngā Kura.

Wylie, C. (2002). *The local and systemic roles of school trustees* [Conference session]. The New Zealand Association for Research in Education Conference, Dunedin, New Zealand, and Palmerston North, New Zealand.

Wylie, C. (2007). *School governance in New Zealand: How is it working?* New Zealand Council for Educational Research. https://www.nzcer.org.nz/research/publications/school-governance-new-zealand-how-it-working

Wylie, C. (2009). Tomorrow's Schools after 20 years: Can a system of self-managing schools live up to its initial aims? *New Zealand Annual Review of Education, 19,* 5–29. https://doi.org/10.26686/nzaroe.v0i19.1555

Wylie, C. & MacDonald, J. (2020). *Trustees' perspectives and the work of school boards—findings from the NZCER 2019 national survey of English-medium primary schools*. New Zealand Council for Educational Research. https://www.nzcer.org.nz/research/publications/trustees-perspectives-and-work-school-boards-findings-nzcer-2019-national

Wylie, C., MacDonald, J., & Tuifagalele, R. (2020). *Women becoming secondary school leaders: Barriers, support, and enablers*. New Zealand Council for Educational Research. http://dx.doi.org/10.18296/rep.0005

Youngs, H. (2005). *Navigating the interface of governance and accountability: A national study of school board chair leadership capability* [Conference session]. The New Zealand Association for Research in Education Conference, Dunedin, New Zealand.

Chapter 3

Solving the Shortage of Principals in Israel by Recruiting Anglo Former Principals

Michael Reichel, Michlalah Jerusalem College, Israel

The school principal is the key driver for promoting student learning (Leithwood et al., 2017). Research has clearly demonstrated that a well-prepared principal is vital for accomplishing deep and sustained achievement for all students (Cherkowski, 2016). The success of educational change inevitably depends on the quality and performance of principals and other school leaders (Hallinger & Heck, 2013).

Despite their critical importance, there is a shortage of good principals. In 2003, a major study concluded that "a shortage of qualified candidates for principal vacancies in the United States exists among rural, urban, and suburban schools, and in elementary, middle, and high schools" (Rosa, 2020). And at about the same time, a respected educator warned that "If your district isn't experiencing a dearth of candidates, it likely will in the near future" (Lovely, 2004, p. 12). The situation has not appreciably improved worldwide (Levin et al., 2019).

This chapter addresses the crisis of principal shortages in Israel and provides a partial solution. The chapter is based on a qualitative study of thirty new immigrants to Israel who had previously been principals at Jewish schools in the United States, England, and Australia. The chapter begins by highlighting the problem and causes of the shortage of qualified principals in Israel. Then, the chapter presents summaries of the study the author conducted that indicate the need for dedicated programs to recruit principals in Israel.

The author of this chapter, himself a former American principal who transitioned to a principalship at a Jerusalem, Israel, school, argues that immigrant administrators, with a proper orientation program, have much to contribute to the Israeli educational system. The chapter outlines the elements of a professional development program for new immigrant principals and other suggestions that could significantly assist in the hiring of new, qualified principals. Some of the ideas in the chapter may be relevant to other school contexts abroad.

THE SITUATION IN ISRAEL

In Israel, the situation reflects the worldwide dearth of qualified school principals (Hine, 2013). This situation remains, to this day, an intractable problem within the Israeli educational system. Indeed, the turnover of principals is substantial worldwide (Levin & Bradley, 2019).

The Capstones Institute, an initiative of the Israeli Ministry of Education that recognizes the vital role of school principals, has found that within Israel's state schools, an average of 207 principals retired every year between 2001 and 2009, while within the smaller state religious school system, an average of sixty-seven principals retired every year. These numbers are in addition to principals who were on scheduled sabbatical or unpaid leave (Capstones, 2012). Luboshitz (2018) reported that between the years 2005 and 2015 the average number of positions opened due to retirement and scheduled sabbatical or paid leave was 552, and in the year 2018, unofficially, there were six hundred open positions.

The total number of state religious schools in Israel is approximately seven hundred fifty, with four hundred fifty elementary schools and three hundred high schools. The head of the state religious school system from 2011–2020, Dr. Avraham Lifshitz stated in a personal interview that over one hundred principals need to be replaced every year in his sector. The shortage of qualified male principals is especially acute in the religious sector. Religious schools are generally divided by gender due to religious requirements among Orthodox Jews. Male principals serving male elementary, middle, and high school students are therefore in great demand.

Recently, Moshe Weinstock, a past chairperson of pedagogy for the Israeli Ministry of Education, stated in a personal interview that his data indicate that approximately seven hundred new principals are needed each year in Israel. Weinstock emphasized that Capstones accepts three hundred candidates for their leadership program annually, but only approximately one hundred graduates actually apply for principal positions. The Capstones Institute confirmed Weinstock's figures, but added that additional graduates of the yearlong course subsequently fill principalships within a few years. The organization estimates that a total of one hundred fifty out of a cohort of three hundred ultimately enter the principalship.

SHORTAGES ABOUND

Recent data regarding Israeli hiring and retention of qualified principals indicate that the problem persists (Shenhav et al., 2021). The need to recruit and retain high-quality school leaders is widely acknowledged by policymakers. To add potential applicants to the current and future pool of principals, the Ministry of Education has created programs to recruit candidates from leadership positions in the army, from individuals in informal education, and from those in leadership positions not related to education.

All of these applicants are required to obtain a teacher's license and accrue several years of experience. Unfortunately, the Ministry of Education has not been successful in filling all the required vacancies (Luboshitz, 2018). As a result, every year hundreds of schools are left without personnel to fill the leadership vacancies left by those retiring or on a sabbatical leave.

Due to the shortage of potential candidates, principalships are often filled by underqualified candidates who are temporarily appointed as acting principals in the hope that the candidates will complete the requirements shortly after undertaking the position. Anecdotally, this author heard about an acting principal who had been approached less than two months before the start of the school year and was asked to apply for the principal position. He was told that, notwithstanding his lack of proper degrees or requirements, he would be allowed to complete the requirements over the next few years.

An additional report circulated among principals: A senior person involved with the interviewing of principals in a large school district stated that most openings for religious elementary schools had just two or three candidates and that many of those were not appropriate for the position. Generally, 75% of applicants were viewed negatively and deemed unqualified to be appointed as principals.

Luboshitz's (2018) research supports the findings that many municipalities have few or even no candidates for their principal openings. These schools get by with either assistant principals or acting principals. Luboshitz does not offer official numbers, but he confirms that schools feel forced to accept candidates who fall short of the requirements.

Similarly, a person who sits on many of the public interview committees stated that in the state school system principal positions draw approximately three to four candidates, while there are even fewer in the state religious school system. There are some positions that draw no appropriate candidates at all, and others have applicants who are not eligible based on the criteria. In 2017 it was disclosed that approximately one-third of open positions were temporarily filled by appointing an acting principal and not via the official channels (Luboshitz, 2018).

CAUSES OF THE SHORTAGES

Internationally, the average age of school principals has been rising over the past two decades, with more than 27% of principals currently over the age of sixty-five and approaching retirement age (Pont et al., 2008). Exacerbating this situation, Pont et al. (2008) warn that in the coronavirus era, schools could face an even greater principal shortage, as older principals opt for early retirement due to health concerns.

Aside from aging principals, fewer applicants are qualified. A 2003 study found that in the United States 55% of school districts reported a shortage of qualified candidates for high school and middle school principal positions, while 47% reported a shortage of elementary candidates (Gordon, 2003). Moreover, of the twenty-two educational systems participating in the OECD's "Improving School Leadership Project," fifteen reported difficulties finding enough suitable candidates for principalships (Pont et al., 2008). In a 2009 survey of 176 American school superintendents, many respondents rated the overall quality of principal candidates as poor (Kwan & Walker, 2009).

Compounding the problem is that fewer educators are interested in the position. Studies from several countries show that most teachers and assistant principals are not interested in moving up to the principalship, since the small additional financial reward does not adequately reflect the large increase in workload and responsibility. In some countries, a lack of career development opportunities may act as a further disincentive for younger people to take on the principalship (Pont et al., 2008).

More specifically, the experience in Israel indicates there are at least three major factors that often deter people from becoming principals: 1) the role is stressful, 2) salaries are not commensurate with the magnitude of responsibilities, and 3) an onerous bureaucracy exists within the Ministry of Education (Hancock et al., 2019; Shenhav et al., 2021).

1. Stress: Researchers have found that the most dissuading factor inhibiting the decision to enter school leadership was the perceived stress that accompanied the position. Common inhibiting factors are work-related stress, loss of contact with children, dealing with difficult parents and teachers, loss of personal time, increased accountability and

expectations, and a salary that is not equal to job expectations (related to point #2).

Stress was reported as a top concern by teachers and teacher leaders in numerous other studies as well (Grissom et al., 2015). The most frequently mentioned factors were less time at home with friends and family; the stress involved; increased responsibility for mandates imposed by local, state, and federal governmental bodies; and ongoing accountability for conditions beyond their personal or professional control (related to point #3).

2. Salaries: The stark fact is that salary differentials (including fringe benefits) in the public sector between teachers and principals are not very significant; thus, the incentives for becoming a principal are minimal (Shenhav et al., 2021). The lack of financial incentives despite the increased workload is a concern. The demand on the principal's time is onerous.

   Principals in some countries work upwards of fifty-four to eighty hours each week, including evenings and weekends (Lovely, 2004). Also, principals generally work eleven months of the year, whereas teachers generally work nine months of the year. Yet, the additional time required in an administration position is typically not offset by adequate compensation. Indeed, there is little financial incentive to become a principal.

3. Bureaucracy: The educational bureaucracry in Israel is manifest, pervasive, and widely perceived as negative (Katz, 2017). In a recent study, school bureaucracy within the confines of a top-down board of education (called The Ministry of Education in Israel) was the most discouraging factor acknowledged by all study participants (Shenhav et al., 2021).

THE RESEARCH STUDY AND A POSSIBLE SOLUTION

This author's research and experience indicate that there is a neglected resource that may alleviate the dearth of principals in Israel almost immediately. It is proposed that Israel recruit former administrators from the Jewish Diaspora. These professionals already have most of the prerequisites and practical experience to lead schools. While cultures and environments are different, these intelligent, well-prepared, experienced leaders could fill the very leadership gap described by Leithwood et al. (2020) as an international concern.

Indeed, there may be a significant number of potential candidates: the vice president of employment for *Nefesh b'Nefesh* (an organization that assists

Anglos to transition to life in Israel), Rachel Berger, said in a private conversation that between 2015 and 2020, thirty-two principals relocated to Israel and 138 people categorized themselves as having worked in educational administration. Experienced principals who wish to contribute to Israeli society have thus been an overlooked resource that could help fill the demand for principals in Israel.

In this study, we assessed the degree to which former Anglo-American principals and assistant principals now living in Israel would be willing to serve as principals in the Israeli education system. For the purposes of this chapter, the precise details of this study are not as important as are the findings and recommendations to help alleviate the shortage of Israeli principals.

Thirty former school administrators were interviewed. Among the study's participants, 80% were male and 20% female. Of the participants, 78% served as principals in the Diaspora in religious K–8 and 9–12 schools, and 22% were assistant principals. Of the males in the group, 93% were ordained rabbis.

Among the study's participants, 31% of participants held doctorates, 56% in educational administration and 54% in general education; 61% held master's degrees and 5.5% possessed only a bachelor's degree. At the time of *aliyah* (immigration to Israel and becoming an Israeli citizen), 17% of participants in this study were above fifty-five years of age and 83% were below that age. All participants moved to Israel for Zionist reasons: While 85% reported religious Zionism as their driving factor, 15% classified themselves as secular Zionists.

Data were collected through semi-structured in-depth interviews, where the interviewer developed and used an "interview guide" but also responded to the situation at hand, to the "emerging worldview of the respondent, and to new ideas on the topic" (Merriam, 2009, p. 90). Key questions were preplanned, but the interviews were also conversational, with questions flowing from previous responses when possible.

Quantitative data analysis for this preliminary study was basic, relying on the use of descriptive statistics. The qualitative data analysis included a four-stage process: condensing, coding, categorizing, and theorizing (Miles et al., 2014).

FINDINGS

Although there were several research questions, including exploring the perceived barriers for entry into the Israeli principalship, discussion here will focus on the second research question, What program can be established to facilitate the inclusion of Anglo immigrants as leaders in Israeli schools?

Despite the various difficulties study participants felt about entering the Israeli educational system, they believed that positive steps could be taken to ease their entry into the local schools. Many suggestions focused on the differences in school cultures between the United States and Israel, such as the role of the principal.

In Israel, principals are considered peers with teachers despite a bit more authority in decision-making. In the United States, principals are given much more authority across a variety of areas. Study participants also highlighted their lack of understanding of the local school system in such matters as curricular requirements and interactions with the teachers union. They considered these to be important items for inclusion in any acculturation program. Representative responses included the following:

- "An intensive Hebrew-language course that [includes] educational jargon is necessary."
- "A mentorship program with principals in a few different schools to learn Israeli leadership styles is critical."
- "Seminars describing the educational philosophy and hierarchy of the Ministry of Education would be helpful."
- "A meeting with youth to understand their language, culture, experiences, and needs is necessary."
- "Meetings with retired Israeli principals would provide deep insights to acculturate us to the system."
- "A one-year internship as an assistant to the principal would help many of us acclimate to the challenges of school leadership here."
- "We would want an explanation of the extent and expectations of parental involvement."
- "Knowing the legal mandates within the ministry is required."
- "An understanding of the extent of rights given to students and parents is important."
- "We would need supervised on-site visits to several schools."
- "Meetings with administrators to show the daily, weekly, monthly, and yearly plans and flow of events . . . is crucial."
- "Meetings with current or former principals who previously made *aliyah* and worked as Israeli principals would be appreciated."
- "Learning about some of the basics is necessary (e.g., how report cards are written, how parent teacher conferences are held, etc.)."
- "An explanation [of] the extent of technological sophistication, differentiated instruction, and other progressive teaching ideas is necessary to become an effective instructional leader."

- "Understanding the workings, political and otherwise, of the Ministry of Education and its policies is fundamental to our ability to navigate the educational system."

Given their extensive experience in school leadership, many study participants said that they would have a great deal to offer the school system in their new home. Their concern was about receptiveness to their involvement. They all felt that they would need support to succeed, but they were confident that they would contribute much. Those participants younger than fifty-five who arrived in Israel were especially optimistic and willing to serve as administrators in the state schools if given an appropriate chance. Those respondents who were no longer eligible to work as principals because of age limitations stated that they would have immigrated earlier had employment as a principal been a realistic option.

Thus, there is reason to believe that new immigrants with educational leadership experience can help solve the problem of the dearth of principals in Israel. An effective program to implement this solution is recommended and should contain several components. First, there should be a program of acculturation, as these leaders have no experience in Israeli classrooms and schools.

A second component of addressing the crisis of a lack of principals is mentoring and induction. Based on Lovely (2004), coaches, veteran mentors, and buddy programs should be standard fare in such a program. Although we are discussing veteran administrators, they would gain immensely from meeting with mentors and from learning about the practical aspects of the local scene such as politics, unions, local and central boards, the balance between strong leadership and governance, and decision-making. Indeed, following Glazer (2000), an additional benefit of this mentoring process would be that it allows future principals to establish important contacts with relevant staff in the state's educational hierarchy.

As with administrative novices, experienced people would be eased into the system as they learned local mores. They would benefit from opportunities to apply known theoretical constructs to new real-life challenges and to focus on authentic problems of practice (Adams & Muthiah, 2020). An additional element of the program's design, per Glazer (2000), would be providing many and varied opportunities for connecting the practical with the theoretical aspects of the profession.

Informed by Glanz (2012), the guidance and tutelage of an assigned advisor or supervisor who would plan, observe, and provide feedback during the "internship" would be important for developing their overall Israeli skill set. The mentor, advisor, and intern could collaboratively plan a detailed program that would provide the intern with a variety of activities (perhaps modeled along lines suggested by New York's Bank Street College Progressive Leadership Program).

In accordance with Glazer (2000), this collaboration would be valuable in that it would ensure that the mentee would gain experience and competency in carefully chosen areas such as school governance, curriculum development, planning, fiscal management, assessment and evaluation of children and staff, human relations, plant management, technology, guidance and pupil personnel services, and Ministry of Education regulations.

Other suggestions such as weekly conference group meetings are also a valuable component of principal internships that can be easily implemented. These forums, for interns and experienced school personal alike, would be very useful for problem-solving, sharing anecdotes, reporting on successes and failures, obtaining guidance and advice, exploring attitudes, dealing with anxieties, and in general receiving collegial support (Glazer, 2000).

RECOMMENDATIONS

To create an appropriate program to help experienced Diaspora principals successfully transition to the Israeli school system (whether they have already immigrated or are considering doing so), a shift in philosophy of the Ministry of Education is necessary. There must be a greater openness to acclimating these experienced men and women with necessary programs implemented to provide support.

A person within the Ministry of Education could be charged with such a recruitment effort. Ideally, this individual should have experience as a principal in a Diasporic environment as well as having served as a principal in Israel. Without attention to such a recruitment effort, an invaluable resource to fill Israeli principal vacancies would be lost.

Most participants in this study mentioned two reasons for their decision not to continue their careers in Jewish education at Israeli schools: 1) a self-perceived weakness of fluency in the spoken language; and 2) cultural differences between the Jewish elementary, middle, or high school in the United States (a private independent school) and the Israeli public school (which operates within a centralized and rigidly constructed framework). Accordingly, a comprehensive, multipronged, two-stage program to recruit Anglo educators to the Israeli school system should include the following:

Stage 1: Recruit Anglo administrators and other experienced educators who are interested in immigration. Currently, many such people do not immigrate because they feel that they would not be able to find employment in their new country in their given field of expertise. A robust recruitment program would include additional survey research, outreach to various Anglo communities, and other strategies such as sharing success stories.

Stage 2: A well-designed professional development program (PD) as well as an acclimation program should be created and implemented for prospective principals in their country of origin. Once their immigration is complete, the program should continue to deepen the skills and knowledge-base of these prospective principals for induction into local schools. This PD initiative would include a thoughtful, relevant, and comprehensive curriculum matched to the skills necessary for them to succeed as school administrators in their new home.

Although the purpose of this chapter is not to articulate a specific PD program, it is advisable to outline some of its key elements. First, it should be noted that some candidates may not be ready to transition into a principalship in Israel, but placing them in teaching positions would be an invaluable experience to acclimate them to the Israeli system. These qualified candidates would also receive a principal mentor to teach them the ins and outs of assuming leadership positions in the Israeli system.

In addition, each candidate should undergo an extensive interview process to ascertain their abilities to become school leaders in Israel. This effort would be monitored by the person in charge within the Ministry of Education, as mentioned above. Other agencies such as Nefesh b'Nefesh and the Jewish Agency, whose roles are to recruit immigrants to Israel, could be helpful in recruiting future school leaders.

Key elements of the PD curriculum should include the following:

- an extensive Hebrew language course geared to the levels of the candidates and to help familiarize them with the professional language they will need
- seminars about all aspects (educational, cultural, financial, curricular, etc.) of the Israeli school system as well as about the nuances of the Ministry of Education
- seminars regarding the duties and responsibilities of school principals and other leadership positions in Israel
- creation of an intensive mentorship and induction program for these candidates prior to their assuming a position, extending over the first three years of their employment

CONCLUSION

The worldwide shortage of properly prepared principals (Potter, 2001) is also a challenge in Israel. This chapter indicated that while hundreds of potential positions are available every year, the Ministry of Education is not able to find qualified candidates for all of them. Efforts to recruit noneducators to fill the positions have been only partially successful.

The interviews of immigrants confirmed that there is a cadre of principals who have already immigrated to Israel, who already have the background and experience that the job requires, and who would be interested in working as administrators in Israeli schools. The analysis of these facts suggests that the Ministry of Education should explore alternative methods of recruiting principals, as described herein. Moreover, professional development programs should be established to recruit diasporic administrators who possess the professional competencies necessary to serve as principals in Israel.

REFERENCES

Adams, D., & Muthiah, V. (2020). School principals and 21st century leadership challenges: A systematic review. *Journal of Nusantara Studies*, 5(1), 189–210.

Capstones. (2012). *School principals reflected in the data*. Jerusalem: Capstones.

Cherkowski, S. (2016). Exploring the role of the school principal in cultivating a professional learning climate. *Journal of School Leadership*, 26(3), 523–543.

De La Rosa, S. (2020). *Report: Nearly half of principals considering leaving their schools*. K–12 Dive. https://www.k12dive.com/news/report-nearly-half-of-principals-considering-leaving-their-schools/577843/

Glanz, J. (2012). *Improving instructional quality in Jewish day schools and yeshivot: Best practices culled from research and the field*. Azrieli Graduate School, Yeshiva University.

Glazer, B. G. (2000). *The preparation of school principals: A study of the Bank Street College Principals Institute*. New York University.

Gordon, G. (2003). *Help wanted: School principals*. The Gallup Organization.

Grissom, J. A., Loeb, S., & Mitani, H. (2015). Principal time management skills: Explaining patterns in principals' time use, job stress, and perceived effectiveness. *Journal of Educational Administration*, 53(6), 773–793.

Hallinger, P., & Heck, R. H. (2013). Leadership and student learning outcomes. In J. Robertson & H. Timperly (Eds.), *Leadership and learning* (pp. 1–17). SAGE Publications.

Hancock, D. R., Müller, U., Wang, C., & Hachen, J. (2019). Factors influencing school principals' motivation to become principals in the USA and Germany. *International Journal of Educational Research*, 95, 90–96.

Hine, G. (2013). Are American schools facing a shortage of qualified administrators? *Journal of Catholic Education, 7*(2), 8.

Katz, Y. J. (2017). Religious education in the Israeli state school system. In M. Sivasubramaniam & R. Hayhoe (Eds.), *Religion and education: Comparative and international perspectives* (pp. 251–270). Oxford.

Kwan, P., & Walker, A. (2009). Are we looking through the same lens? Principal recruitment and selection. *International Journal of Educational Research, 48*(1), 51–61.

Leithwood, K., Harris, A., & Hopkins, D. (2020). Seven strong claims about successful school leadership revisited. *School Leadership and Management, 40*(1), 5–22.

Leithwood, K., Sun, J., & Pollock, K. (Eds.). (2017). *How school leaders contribute to student success: The four paths framework* (vol. 23). Springer.

Levin, S., & Bradley, K. (2019). Understanding and addressing principal turnover: A review of the research. National Association of Secondary School Principals, Learning Policy Institute. https://learningpolicyinstitute.org/product/nassp-understanding-addressing-principal-turnover-review-research-report

Levin, S., Bradley, K., & Scott, C. (2019). Principal turnover: Insights from current principals. National Association of Secondary School Principals, Learning Policy Institute. https://learningpolicyinstitute.org/product/nassp-principal-turnover-insights-brief

Lovely, S. (2004). *Staffing the principalship: Finding, coaching, and mentoring school leaders.* Association for Supervision and Curriculum Development.

Luboshitz, T. (2018). *Minui menahalim be-ma'arechet ha'chinuch* [Appointing principals in the Israeli education system]. Forum Kohelet.

Merriam, S. B. (2009). *Qualitative research: A guide to design and implementation.* Jossey-Bass.

Miles, M. B., Huberman, M. A., & Saldana, J. (2014). *Qualitative data analysis: A methods sourcebook.* SAGE Publications.

Pont, B., Nusche, D., & Moorman, H. (2008). *Improving school leadership, Volume 1: Policy and practice.* OECD Publishing.

Potter, L. (2001). Solving the principal shortage. *Principal, 80*(4), 34–37.

Shenhav, S., Geffon, A., Salomon, L., & Glanz, J. (2021). Encouraging and discouraging factors in the decision to become an Israeli leader in religious schools: Implications for reforming bureaucratic mandates of the Ministry of Education. *International Journal of Educational Reform, 30*(1), 77–97.

Chapter 4

Strengthening Educational Leadership Preparation Programs to Better Prepare Principals to Aid Retention

Kathleen M. W. Cunnigham, Henry Tran, Suzy Hardie, Tammy S. Taylor, and Renice K. Sauls, University of South Carolina

Supporting the development and practice of pre-service and in-service school principals requires close attention to the structures, experiences, and supports for their leadership growth. This chapter focuses on strategies for faculty in university-based educational leadership preparation programs (LPPs) to consider, to employ both during the preparation program experience and post-program induction and support.

We draw from extant literature on effective leadership preparation programming (Cunningham et al., 2019; Crow & Whiteman, 2016; Fusarelli et al., 2019; Merchant & Garza, 2015; Orr, 2011; Snodgrass Rangel, 2018; VanGronigen et al., 2019; Young, 2015; Young et al., 2021) and qualitative interview data we collected from practicing principals to identify opportunities to encourage their success and to promote their retention in the field.

This chapter will describe different ways educational leadership preparation programs can integrate powerful learning experiences (PLEs) (Young, 2015; Young et al., 2021) within their coursework to support aspiring leaders across their career stages, from leadership development and training, to their hire and eventual flourishing in their roles as school leaders. While causality or guarantee that the inclusion of specific preparation program elements will impact retention cannot be claimed, we focus on a subset of high-leverage evidence-based preparation program characteristics that offer promising potential.

Research suggests these are effective when developing high-quality school leaders by preparing them in a way that encourages success, self-efficacy, and growth in their role.

This chapter first discusses educational leadership turnover and retention, and why attention to this topic is of critical importance. Then, we outline some typical elements that educational leadership preparation program faculty focus upon when engaged in program design and execution. Lastly, we explore characteristics of powerful learning experiences that preparation faculty can incorporate when designing coursework and supporting leaders beyond the program to promote their success and retention.

WHY IS THE RETENTION OF SCHOOL LEADERS IMPORTANT?

It is estimated that principal turnover is almost 20% every year (Goldring & Taei, 2018), and Bartanen et al. (2019) suggest that principal turnover rates eclipse the rates of teacher turnover, the latter of which is an issue that frequently receives the bulk of media and policy attention. Principal turnover is costly. From a financial perspective, replacing a school principal can cost anywhere from 25% to more than 50% of the principal's salary, depending on who and what is involved in the replacement process (Tran et al., 2018).

Furthermore, while the departure of ineffective principals can be beneficial for schools, frequent turnover of principals negatively impacts the academic experience of students, as reflected in declines in student achievement (Bartanen et al., 2019). This negative causal effect is theorized to operate through disruption of academic continuity, loss of leadership experience, and inconsistency of school direction that results from principal changes.

While it takes a school leader approximately five years to implement a vision for the school and positively affect the culture (Weinstein et al., 2009), research shows that, on average, principals turn over every four years (Bartanen & Grissom, 2021), resulting in a constant churn of unfulfilled potential. Furthermore, principal turnover is statistically linked to teacher turnover (Bartanen et al., 2019). This may be because teachers follow their departing principals to a new district or school, or it could be that the organizational instability from principal turnover motivates teachers to leave. This can be particularly harmful for students. As Tekleselassie and Choi (2021) explain, "[f]requent administrator turnover may fuel teacher turnover, further damaging the educational gains and benefits of the neediest group of the population where a stable leadership (and teaching force) is found to make the most impact" (p. 1142).

WHY DO PRINCIPALS LEAVE?

Based on twelve years of longitudinal data from North Carolina, Miller (2013) found that principals leave after a downturn in school performance and that performance continues to fall two years after the position is filled by a replacement. Grissom and Bartanen's (2019) analysis of 14 years of longitudinal data from Tennessee elaborated on those findings by showing that those principals who are both the least and most effective are more likely to leave: the former group is likely to be reassigned to other lower-level school positions, while those in the latter group are more likely to move to district-level positions. Some districts rotate principals to different schools, but doing so can potentially put the school's continuity and academic performance at risk (Bartanen et al., 2019).

Salaries also play an important role in principal turnover. Tran and Buckman (2017) found that principals who left their district to lead schools in other districts earned higher salaries than those who stayed, and the researchers surmised that the opportunity for higher pay likely influenced their departure. Tran's (2017) work also linked principals' feelings about their pay to their turnover intentions; specifically, principals who are less satisfied with their pay are more likely to want to leave their position. Noticeably, their levels of satisfaction are influenced by the relative salaries of their peers (i.e., other teachers in their district, other principals within their district and, most importantly, principals in other districts).

In a comprehensive review of the literature on principal turnover, Snodgrass Rangel (2018) found that the strongest determinants of principal turnover included low school performance and the implementation of accountability systems (e.g., principals may leave low-income/urban schools particularly when categorized as "failing"). That said, strong professional development (PD) was found to mitigate turnover and improve retention (Jacob et al., 2015), suggesting that strengthening LPP support holds promise for keeping principals in schools.

UNIVERSITY-BASED EDUCATIONAL LEADERSHIP PREPARATION

University-based educational leadership preparation programs (LPPs) provide professional development to individuals seeking educational administration roles, such as the school principalship. Although LPPs look different across institutions and are beholden to state policies that vary in their requirements (Anderson & Reynolds, 2015), exemplary LPPs design and continuously improve upon a coherent sequence of courses and clinical or internship experiences that contain PLE opportunities (Cosner, 2019).

The University Council for Educational Administration's (UCEA) Institutional and Program Quality Criteria (Young et al., 2012) suggest that K–12 educational leadership preparation programs should attend to the following areas: engaging faculty members to "identify, develop, and promote relevant knowledge of best practices focused on the essential problems of schooling, leadership, and administration" (p. 3); fostering program partnerships; supporting candidates during their clinical practices, developing and continuously improving upon a coherent and authentic program curriculum; and providing support that continues beyond the program itself to also include support of in-service school leaders (see p. 3).

As pre-service leaders move into in-service leadership roles, they are typically hired in an assistant principal (AP) position and later move into the principalship (Goldring et al., 2021; Jackson & Kelly, 2002). LPP graduates will encounter myriad experiences while in their AP role; some of which might align to what they learned in their preparation, and others—such as socialization, policy constraints, or drastic changes in the educational landscape—that may impact their careers in different ways (Oleszewski et al., 2012).

Consider leadership preparation Program A. Program A develops aspiring leaders by building their capacity to engage in conversations about issues of equity and lead necessary changes or disrupt current practices to make schooling more equitable for students, particularly those who are most marginalized (e.g., students of color, English language learners, students with refugee status, students in special education). One graduate from Program A feels nervous, but confident she will be able to facilitate meaningful equity work in the new school where she was recently hired as an assistant principal. Early in her time as an AP, however, she is regularly discouraged by her principal from engaging in direct equity improvement work because the principal feels that the staff are "not ready to engage with those topics and conversations" and "don't need parents calling the school." Disconnects like the one described in this scenario as well as other socialization elements may deny the AP on-the-job development opportunities or may contribute to a stymieing of the work she wants to engage in. These issues may even prevent or slow her career progression (Oleszewski et al., 2012).

Faculty in LPPs can confront situations such as this within their programs. They are positioned to give a "heads-up" to their aspiring leaders about potential pushbacks or disconnects. Creating opportunities for aspiring leaders to authentically reflect on and plan for how they might navigate these types of values-based challenges during course or clinical work is one way to help them practice prior to assuming their roles. Best practices in leadership preparation programming, such as authentic and coherent program design, can help program faculty incorporate impactful learning activities.

Activities intentionally designed for this purpose can provide opportunities for students to grapple with authentic problems of practice while also being directly supported as they develop their leadership. Young et al. (2021) outline ten attributes of PLEs that signal the presence of high-quality program activities to university faculty.

While these PLEs were identified by Young et al. for the purposes of preparing aspiring school administrators to lead from day one in a leadership role, for this chapter, we consider how preparation programs might prepare aspiring leaders to lead over time (i.e., before and during their leadership role). The ten PLE characteristics are as follows:

1. *Authentic*: The activity is directly connected and relevant to future leadership practice.
2. *Active*: The activity invites engagement on addressing an authentic problem of practice, bridging theory to practice, etc.
3. *Sensemaking*: The activity encourages aspiring leaders to engage in sensemaking, grappling with a problem of practice or an educational issue.
4. *Centers equity*: The activity calls on aspiring leaders to "explore, critique, and deconstruct problems, beliefs, practices, and policies from an equity perspective" (p. 4).
5. *Reflective*: The activity includes purposeful space for reflection on one's leadership.
6. *Collaboration and interdependence*: The activity is designed to have aspiring leaders engage with one another in various ways to accomplish a task or goal.
7. *Responsibility for learning*: The activity "empowers learners to take responsibility for their own learning" (p. 5).
8. *Learner and knower*: The activity is aligned with adult learning theory (e.g., Knowles, 1973) and provides everyone in the class (including the preparation program instructor and the aspiring leaders) with a learning mindset (i.e., learners may continually learn and improve their skill sets over time).
9. *Broadens perspective*: The activity requires aspiring leaders to widen their perspectives and decision-making considerations from the classroom to the whole school, the district, and the state level of the system.
10. *Confidence building*: The activity increases the confidence and efficacy of the aspirants.

Purposeful attention to incorporating all of the above PLEs when designing an LPP curriculum could enhance opportunities for aspiring leaders to prepare for the formal role of school leader, as the LPP is designed to increase their sense of self efficacy–a critical factor in retention (e.g., Tschannen-Moran & Gareis, 2004). When multiple characteristics are used collectively, PLEs support future school leaders to be adaptive to their contexts, communities, needs, and challenges (Cunningham et al., 2019).

LPPS AND RETENTION: RECOMMENDATIONS FOR PREPARATION AND INDUCTION

We conducted a qualitative interview study (Tran et al., 2022 that collected the perspectives of in-service principals in rural schools who identify as Black women ($n = 7$). We selected illustrative interview data that highlight why they stay in educational leadership. Notably, several participants were raised in the community where they currently work as principals and have a deep connection to it.

For these leaders, this factor was identified as a reason motivating them to work in their schools. This connects to prior research on "grow your own" programs and may hold implications for LPP partnerships and recruitment considerations (Merchant & Garza, 2015). Further, the participants' professional experiences related to leadership development signal where LPPs can improve to make preparation and leadership development more effective.

Because educational leadership candidates spend a relatively short time in their preparation program (i.e., one to two years), it is crucial that the time they spend in the program is impactful. Infusing the program with PLEs is a strategy that encourages meaningful learning (Young et al., 2021). A challenge of leadership preparation programs is that, in their short time duration, programs cannot prepare aspiring leaders for the exhaustive list of everything they might encounter in the field.

To summarize what Principal Dottie noted in her interview, until someone is a school leader, one cannot know how to do everything the position demands. This suggests that leadership learning and development should continue after the formal LPP experience concludes, and also suggests that there is an opportunity for LPPs to support recent graduates through induction programs.

Research on new teacher induction offers promising evidence of how induction programs can support teacher retention (e.g., Skeen, 2019). Similarly, university-based leadership induction could provide newly minted leaders with guidance and support during their first years in administration, especially for those scenarios that the formal preparation program could not address.

In considering what LPP faculty can offer aspiring and novice educational leaders, it is worth exploring how PLE characteristics are incorporated into the program. While each PLE characteristic is important, for the purposes of this chapter we highlight only a sample of PLEs that we anticipate will align well with supporting school leaders' retention.

We suggest how PLE 1 (makes authentic connections to leadership), PLE 4 (centers equity), PLE 6 (involves collaboration and interdependence), and PLE 10 (builds confidence) (Young et al., 2021), can all be incorporated both during and after program completion. We use existing literature and the study participants' (i.e., in-service leaders') perspectives to make connections to these sample PLE characteristics.

PLE 1: Makes Authentic Connection to Leadership

During the Preparation Program. Myriad considerations need attention when LPP faculty design a curriculum that effectively meets aspiring school principals' needs and helps them to develop the courage to advocate for all students and work with their staff to dismantle systemic systems of oppression. Extant research documents ways university LPPs tailor programs to align with the authentic contexts many of their graduates will lead in after program completion (e.g., Cosner et al., 2015; Merchant & Garza, 2015).

For instance, the University of Illinois Chicago offers a tailored program that incorporates elements of their longtime partner Chicago Public Schools (CPS), such as selection processes and an authentic exploration of espoused district priorities for developing educational leaders who will effectively serve the district's students (Cosner et al., 2015). In our sample, because many of our participants noted they stayed at their schools to lead in the communities where they grew up, LPP faculty can intentionally design learning experiences to incorporate real and authentic contextual considerations of the districts where their aspiring administrators hope to lead.

In addition to contextual applicability, learning experiences can invite real-world applicability through reviewing work of current school leaders. Examples may include analyzing sample data from a school, helping an existing school-based team to address a problem of practice, or using a school's work or improvement plan to analyze to what extent the school's budget aligns with the stated values and vision of their school (Cunningham et al., 2019). Simulations or role-playing of a realistic problem or conversation are other ways to practice navigating authentic leadership dilemmas (Orr et al., 2013).

Providing leaders with varied experiences that are directly related to their future work can build the capacity of new leaders to navigate challenges successfully (Young et al., 2021). The internship is a prime opportunity to do this. One principal interview participant suggested LPPs should require students to shadow principals for longer periods of time, since day-to-day work can change so dramatically. A more holistic internship experience can demonstrate the reality of the job's cadence and better inform aspiring principals, so they feel more comfortable to not only survive, but thrive in their roles.

During Induction. Teacher induction incorporates mentoring to support new teachers because "[m]any enter the profession with the tools and knowledge required for success. However, new teachers often find themselves at a loss for how to effectively wield these tools" (Skeen, 2019, para. 2).

In a parallel way, one interview participant, an elementary principal named Abigail, noted there was no transition program provided to her when she moved into the role of school principal. She talked about the challenges of not having support during that transition. LPP faculty can continue their relationship with their students by providing in-service leaders with structured mentoring times to debrief and reflect on the leadership challenges that arise for the novice principal.

Another principal, Tara, shared that she felt as if she was expected "to know everything," simply because she held the formal role of principal. This is an unrealistic and unfair expectation of her and even minimizes the continuous improvement and professional growth mindset and opportunities. That said, structured mentoring or coaching by university faculty could continue to bridge theory to practice related to something the novice leader is currently facing—thus directly impacting leadership development and supporting principals in improving their professional practice. This would have met the direct needs of Georgia, a principal who commented that "as a rural principal, having a mentor would have been really helpful." This type of induction support could be forwarded by programmatic structures and organizations, or internal/external funding (e.g., grants).

PLE 4: Centers Equity

During the Preparation Program. According to the interview participants, critical reasons for remaining in educational leadership were their values and their relationships with students and teachers. When asked what kept her in her role, Principal Georgia replied, "Definitely the students and wanting to be here for the teachers. . . . I saw so many problems that I wanted to try and help solve. That has been the thing that really kept me here because I wanted to see it done right or see it done successfully."

Principal Dottie shared in her interview that it is important for young students to see someone who looked like them in a leadership position, "for little Black girls to be able to say, 'Well [Principal Dottie] did it. Why can't I?'"

When LPPs help aspiring leaders make connections to their "why" and what they value, those connections will shape who they are as leaders, and guide their decisions and how they reflect on their practice. Connecting values to LPP learning experiences can be realized by connecting opportunities for critical examination of what qualitative and quantitative data reveal (or do not reveal) to potential action steps.

Further, it is important to provide spaces for aspiring leaders to learn what it looks like to leverage data to guide school priority areas while focusing on strengths and assets, not deficits. Practicing asset-based data use will invite aspiring leaders to begin to identify opportunities to make schooling more equitable for students (Honig & Walsh, 2019).

During Induction. Principal Georgia noted that her district does not offer districtwide, culturally relevant activities and it is "left up to you as a school if you're going to do anything that honors a different set of cultures and values. You have to figure it out on your own." Principal Georgia's comment reveals an opportunity for LPPs. If equity and culturally responsive pedagogy and leadership (Khalifa, 2018) are included during leader preparation, new leaders may have promising ideas for guiding their schools in culturally responsive ways and through an asset-based lens (e.g., Gay, 2002; McKenzie & Scheurich, 2004). Continued LPP support during leaders' induction into their roles can provide resources, best practices, and strategies for them to boldly lead with an equity lens while receiving ongoing support and mentoring.

PLE 6: Involves Collaboration and Interdependence

During the Preparation Program. Programs need to encourage aspiring leaders to be reflective about their leadership and collaboration style. In her experience, Principal Dottie needed to warn a new leader, telling her, "If people see you just walking around here being nasty, they're not going to follow you. That's when you're going to have the pushback, and nobody wants to be here." Principal Dottie summarized, "You can't come in and drop the hammer and not care about people." Practicing collaboration during LPP is particularly important and can be incorporated as part of coursework. Engaging in the important and straining work of educational leadership successfully requires teamwork and trust in collaborative working environments (NPBEA, 2018).

During Induction. Induction opportunities can create time for reflecting with leaders on how they might collaborate with their co-workers. As one principal emphasized, the job of school principal is "massive." Principals who step into the role could benefit from analyzing with LPP faculty how to distribute leadership appropriately and effectively.

This aligns with what Principal Dottie suggested. She recommended that new principals "observe first" and they should not "come in and try to change everything before [they] even start . . . because it's going to mess up climate and culture." Collaboration and observation for learning can be encouraged during mentoring meetings with new leaders to guide when and where organizational improvements can be made.

PLE 10: Builds Confidence

During the Preparation Program. The LLP can incorporate scaffolded opportunities for the aspiring leader to consistently learn and gain confidence in their leadership development. Increasing the confidence of aspiring school leaders is a critical PLE to consider when examining retention. Feeling prepared for a new challenge can increase efficacy and perseverance (Tschannen-Moran & Gareis, 2004; 2007).

During Induction. Principal interviews revealed that leadership development after graduation, when candidates worked in the role of the AP and then principal, was not as regular, supportive, or available as it should have been. Principal Georgia noted that in-service "principals should not feel like they have to reach out to people on Facebook to receive support to do their jobs." Principal Abigail juxtaposed teacher and principal induction, noting new teachers were provided support, but new leaders were not.

Similar to PLE 1 (i.e., authentic connections), leaders' experiences highlight opportunities for university LPPs to engage new leaders in an induction program to help fill this gap and support them to navigate their new role and gain confidence in their decision-making skills. This could be particularly helpful if there is limited or no support from the district.

CONCLUSION

The aforementioned literature captured different factors that influence leaders' decisions to stay at or leave their schools. Certain factors—such as salary (e.g., Tran & Buckman, 2017)—are out of the control of LPPs. Other factors, such as professional development opportunities (Snodgrass Rangel, 2018), are ones LPPs might be able to influence. As the principals who were part of this study helped reveal, LPPs are well-positioned to weave in opportunities to connect to different areas of the work.

The work of educational leaders, including their pre-service and in-service development, is complex. Discussions of educator burnout are very much a part of the national conversation. Burnout is exacerbated by factors such as COVID-19, restrictive educational laws and policies, and increased stress due to the demands on school leaders (DeMatthews, 2021).

Unfortunately, these challenges have not abated. Within our sphere of influence, we hope there are places where we can support leaders in their ongoing practice in the face of professional challenges. In alignment with prior research (Tschannen-Moran & Gareis, 2004; 2007), we argue that feeling prepared for challenges can increase efficacy and perseverance. This preparedness ultimately allows leaders to feel engaged and supported, which are two necessary catalysts for retention. To feel prepared, school leaders must practice navigating various intersections of decision-making.

LPPs can provide opportunities both during the program and beyond the coursework to support the growth of leaders' capacities, skills, and professional habits (e.g., reflection, equitable practice, working collaboratively) and build their capacity for being adaptive (Young et al., 2021). Then, when the leadership role becomes particularly challenging, administrators can lean upon their supports and muscle memory that has been strengthened through practicing and honing skills, and hopefully thrive as principals who remain successful in the field.

It is our hope that this chapter 1) offered entry points for further exploration in this area, and 2) provided guidance for LPP faculty members to incorporate PLEs to help graduates persevere rather than leave when encountering threats of burnout, stress, and organizational changes.

REFERENCES

Anderson, E., & Reynolds, A. L., (2015). *A policymaker's guide: Research-based policy for principal preparation program approval and licensure.* University Council for Educational Administration. http://www.ucea.org/resource/policy-reports/

Bartanen, B., & Grissom, J. A. (2021). School principal race, teacher racial diversity, and student achievement. *Journal of Human Resources*, 0218–9328R2.

Bartanen, B., Grissom, J. A., & Rogers, L. K. (2019). The impacts of principal turnover. *Educational Evaluation and Policy Analysis*, *41*(3), 350–374.

Cosner, S. (2019). What makes a leadership preparation program exemplary? *Journal of Research on Leadership Education*, *14*(1), 98–115.

Cosner, S., Tozer, S., Zavitkovsky, P., & Whalen, S. P. (2015). Cultivating exemplary school leadership preparation at a research intensive university. *Journal of Research on Leadership Education*, *10*(1), 11–38.

Crow, G. M., & Whiteman, R. S. (2016). Effective preparation program features. *Journal of Research on Leadership Education*, *11*(1), 120–148.

Cunningham, K. M. W., VanGronigen, B. A., Tucker, P. D., & Young, M. D. (2019). Using powerful learning experiences to prepare school leaders. *Journal of Research on Leadership Education, 14*(1), 74–97.

DeMatthews, D. (2021, October 21). *We're facing a looming crisis of principal burnout.* Education Week. https://www.edweek.org/leadership/opinion-were-facing-a-looming-crisis-of-principal-burnout/2021/10

Fusarelli, B. C., Fusarelli, L. D., & Drake, T. A. (2019). NC State's principal leadership academies: Context, challenges, and promising practices. *Journal of Research on Leadership Education, 14*(1), 11–30.

Gay, G. (2002). Culturally responsive teaching in special education for ethnically diverse students: Setting the stage. *International Journal of Qualitative Studies in Education, 15*(6), 613–629.

Goldring, R., & Taei, S. (2018). *Principal attrition and mobility: Results from the 2016–17 principal follow-up survey* (Report No. 2018–066). National Center for Education Statistics, U.S. Department of Education.

Goldring, E., Rubin, M., & Herrmann, M. (2021). *The role of assistant principals: Evidence and insights for advancing school leadership. Study highlights.* The Wallace Foundation. https://www.wallacefoundation.org/knowledge-center/Documents/The-Role-of-Assistant-Principals-Evidence-Insights-for-Advancing-School-Leadership-Highlights.pdf

Grissom, J. A., & Bartanen, B. (2019). Principal effectiveness and principal turnover. *Education Finance and Policy, 14*(3), 355–382.

Honig, M. I., & Donaldson Walsh, E. (2019). Learning to lead the learning of leaders: The evolution of the University of Washington's education doctorate. *Journal of Research on Leadership Education, 14*(1), 51–73.

Jackson, B. L., & Kelley, C. (2002). Exceptional and innovative programs in educational leadership. *Educational Administration Quarterly, 38*(2), 192–212.

Jacob, R., Goddard, R., Kim, M., Miller, R., & Goddard, Y. (2015). Exploring the causal impact of the McREL Balanced Leadership Program on leadership, principal efficacy, instructional climate, educator turnover, and student achievement. *Educational Evaluation and Policy Analysis, 37*(3), 314–332.

Khalifa, M. A. (2018). *Culturally responsive school leadership.* Harvard Education Press.

Knowles, M. (1973). *The adult learner: A neglected species.* American Society for Training and Development, Gulf Publishing Company.

McKenzie, K. B., & Scheurich, J. J. (2004). Equity traps: A useful construct for preparing principals to lead schools that are successful with racially diverse students. *Educational Administration Quarterly, 40*(5), 601–632.

Merchant, B., & Garza, E. (2015). The Urban School Leaders Collaborative: Twelve years of promoting leadership for social justice. *Journal of Research on Leadership Education, 10*(1), 39–62.

Miller, A. (2013). Principal turnover and student achievement. *Economics of Education Review, 36*, 60–72.

National Policy Board for Educational Administration (NPBEA). (2018). *National Educational Leadership Preparation (NELP) Program recognition standards: Building level.* https://www.npbea.org/wp-content/uploads/2018/11/NELP-Building-Standards.pdf

Oleszewski, A., Shoho, A., & Barnett, B. (2012). The development of assistant principals: A literature review. *Journal of Educational Administration, 50*(3), 264–286.

Orr, M. T. (2011). Pipeline to preparation to advancement: Graduates' experiences in, through, and beyond leadership preparation. *Educational Administration Quarterly, 47*(1), 114–172.

Orr, M. T., Rorrer, A. K., & Young, M. D. (2013). *Developing evaluation evidence: A formative and summative evaluation planner for educational leadership preparation programs.* Center for the Evaluation of Educational Leadership Preparation and Practice, University Council for Educational Administration. http://www.ucea.org/wp-content/uploads/2014/08/Developing-Evaluation-Evidence-2013.pdf

Skeen, N. (2019). *CarolinaTIP: A promising solution to the teacher shortage.* SC-Teacher. https://sc-teacher.org/nicoleskeen/

Snodgrass Rangel, V. (2018). A review of the literature on principal turnover. *Review of Educational Research, 88*(1), 87–124.

Tekleselassie, A. A., & Choi, J. (2021). Understanding school principal attrition and mobility through hierarchical generalized linear modeling. *Educational Policy, 35*(7), 1116–1162.

Tran, H. (2017). The impact of pay satisfaction and school achievement on high school principals' turnover intentions. *Educational Management Administration & Leadership, 45*(4), 621–638.

Tran, H., & Buckman, D. G. (2017). The impact of principal movement and school achievement on principal salaries. *Leadership and Policy in Schools, 16*(1), 106–129.

Tran, H., Cunningham, K. M., Hardie, S., Taylor, T., & Sauls, R. (2022). Seeing the visibly invisible: An intersectional analysis of the employee experiences of Black female rural educators. *Teachers College Record,* 01614681231153699.

Tran, H., McCormick, J., & Nguyen, T. T. (2018). The cost of replacing South Carolina high school principals. *Management in Education, 32*(3), 109–118.

Tschannen-Moran, M., & Gareis, C. R. (2004). Principals' sense of self-efficacy. *Educational Administration, 42*(5), 573–585.

Tschannen-Moran, M., & Gareis, C. R. (2007). Cultivating principals' self-efficacy: Supports that matter. *Journal of School Leadership, 17*(1), 89–103.

VanGronigen, B. A., Cunningham, K. M. W., & Young, M. D. (2019). How exemplary educational leadership preparation programs hone the interpersonal-intrapersonal (i2) skills of future leaders. *Journal of Transformative Leadership & Policy Studies, 7*(2), 1–11.

Weinstein, M., Schwartz, A. E., Jacobowitz, R., Ely, T., & Landon, K. (2009). *New schools, new leaders: A study of principal turnover and academic achievement at new high schools in New York City* (Research Paper No. 2011-09). New York University Wagner School of Public Service Research Paper Series.

Young, M. D. (2015). The leadership challenge: Supporting the learning of all students. *Leadership and Policy in Schools, 14*, 389–410. doi:10.1080/15700763.2015.1073330

Young, M. D., Cunningham, K. M. W., VanGronigen, B. A., & O'Doherty, A. (2021). Transformational leadership preparation in a post-COVID world: US perspectives. *eJournal of Education Policy, 21*(1), 1–23.

Young, M.D., Tucker, P., & Orr, M.T. (2012). *University Council for Educational Administration (UCEA) institutional and program quality criteria: Guidance for master's and doctoral programs in educational leadership.* UCEA. http://markfavazza.wpenginepowered.com/wp-content/uploads/2014/07/UCEAProgramCriteria.pdf

Chapter 5

We're Hiring, but Will They Come?

The Challenges of Recruiting Racially Diverse Principal Candidates in Rural Schools

Simone A. F. Gause, Coastal Carolina University,
Henry Tran, University of South Carolina
David G. Buckman, Augusta University

The increasing diversity of student demographics is impacting schools and communities across the United States (Frankenberg & Orfield, 2012). As a result, many school districts and administrators have made it a publicly stated priority to have their teaching and school leadership workforces reflect their student population (Tran et al., 2020a; Carter Andrews et al., 2019). The looming question, then, is how do we build a diverse education workforce? While the question endures, it is not a new phenomenon, as educators, administrators, and policy makers have grappled with this challenge with historic and mixed results for decades (Carter Andrews et al., 2019; Putman et al., 2016).

In the United States, researchers have focused comprehensively on understanding the lack of representation of diverse teachers in the education workforce. For instance, scholars have investigated recruiting and retaining teachers of color (Achinstein et.al., 2010; Goings & Bianco, 2016), student outcomes with same-race teachers (Gershenson et.al., 2017; Easton-Brooks et.al, 2009), experiences of students with teachers from similar racial/ethnic backgrounds (Bristol, 2015; Goings & Bianco, 2016), experiences of students of color in teacher preparation programs (Amos, 2016; Sleeter, 2001), in-service experiences of teachers of color (Bristol, 2018; Gist, 2014), retention of teachers of color (Ingersoll et al., 2017), and attrition of teachers of color (Ingersoll et al., 2014).

While research on diversifying the teacher workforce has increased, it is primarily focused on how to recruit more teachers into the profession and understanding why teachers stay or leave. Although this research is important, the scholarly discourse on the importance of diverse school-based leaders or principals in rural school districts is not nearly as extensive, but it is gaining attention from scholars and policymakers (Bartanen & Grissom, 2019; Castro et.al., 2018; Hammond et al., 2001).

The chapter confronts the challenges of hiring principal candidates from diverse backgrounds within the geographical constraints of localities. Specifically, the purposes of this chapter are to highlight the current difficulties recruiting principals from racially diverse backgrounds, especially in rural contexts, and to detail practical, asset-based solutions as mitigating strategies for the staffing struggles. We draw on original data to exemplify the problem and look to the literature and scholarship to provide recommendations to aide in the diversification of school leadership in rural school districts and others like them.

RACIAL DIVERSITY AND RURALITY

Although more than half of US students are racial minorities, about 89.7% of rurally located public school principals are White, according to a 2017–2018 survey data collected by the National Center for Education Statistics (NCES, 2019a). That surpasses the national average of 77.7% of school principals being White. However, these statistics mirror the makeup of the rural American teaching workforce, which is about 90% White (NCES, 2019b), and higher than the national average of 79.3% White. The remaining rural school principals were about 3.1% Hispanic, 4.5% Black and 2.7% other races (NCES, 2019a).

Urban districts were more likely to have principals of color than their rural, town, and suburban counterparts. Gender diversity within rural school leadership reveals that 53.1% of school principals are male, the highest of all school locales, and surpasses the national average of 46.3% of school principals being male (NCES, 2019a). Without implying a direct correlation, males make up only 24.3% the rural teacher workforce (NCES, 2019b).

Previous federal initiatives (e.g., Race to the Top, National Center for Research on Rural Education, National Center for Research on Rural Education Support, Regional Educational Laboratories) recognized the importance of school principals in improving school performance, and particularly in turning around underperforming schools. Programs like Race to the Top emphasized professional development and performance incentive systems to attract, improve, and retain principals. However, scholars and state policymakers are concerned that the principal workforce is aging, is homogeneous, and remains predominantly unchanged despite the changing demographics of the student population (Castro et.al., 2018; Bartanen & Grissom, 2019).

The need for the diversification of the teaching profession has received much attention (Carver-Thomas, 2018; Partelow et al., 2017). This is especially the case given 1) research findings that link teachers of color to positive outcomes for students of color, including not only learning, but also their social and emotional development (Bristol & Martin-Fernandez, 2019); and b) scholarship that suggests negative racialized experiences in the education workplace contribute to the burnout and attrition of Black, Indigenous, people of color (BIPOC) teachers (Achinstein et al., 2010; Mahatmya et al., 2022). Yet much less is known about diversity challenges in education leadership, and calls for diversifying leadership are scant relative to calls for diversifying the teaching body (Carter Andrews et al., 2019).

While many districts have a stated priority for diversifying their teachers' corps, diversifying leadership is often not a stated priority (Buckman & Tran, 2022). This is problematic for several reasons. For instance, like the diversity of teachers, leadership diversity in schools has been linked to positive student outcomes, such as higher representation of underrepresented students of color in gifted programs and improved student learning growth (Bartanen & Grissom, 2021; Grissom & Redding, 2016).

Furthermore, teachers of color who are racially or ethnically matched with their principals are more likely to be satisfied with their jobs and turn over less often (Grissom & Keiser, 2011). Principals of color are also more likely to hire teachers of color (Bartanen & Grissom, 2019). Moreover, the lack of attention to leadership diversification exacerbates and sustains the well-documented existence of the glass ceiling effect, a phenomenon where less diversity is found in higher-paying leadership positions and diversity becomes scarcer as the positions become more prestigious and command a higher salary (Cotter et al., 2001).

FACTORS IMPACTING RURAL PRINCIPAL RECRUITMENT

The principalship has been rendered increasingly unattractive to candidates due to escalating accountability pressures, reduced decision-making authority, and a highly political space involving polarizing communities. Additionally, there is insufficient pay to offset these rising challenges and demands (Doyle & Locke, 2014). Recruiting quality candidates is made even more challenging for many rural schools due to their lower relative salaries, lack of mentoring, increased workload (due to having to wear "multiple hats" in a smaller context with less administrative support), scarce resources, geographic challenges associated with lack of amenities and social scenery, and professional and personal isolation (Cruzeiro & Boone, 2009; Tran et al., 2020b; Wood et al., 2013).

The problem is further compounded when it comes to recruiting principals of color (Lee & Mao, 2020). While many educational organizations and school districts often outwardly state a commitment to fostering diversity within their organizations (Healy, 2016), these efforts do not always translate to successful recruitment campaigns (Buckman & Tran, 2018; Putman et al., 2016). There are internal and external obstacles encountered when recruiting diverse candidates, which can be categorized in four main areas: implicit bias, explicit bias, candidate interest, and geographical limitations.

Implicit Bias

District leaders may recruit for principals by relying on their social networks, and those networks are segregated by race (Grissom & Keiser, 2011; Nzau et al., 2021). Wood et al. (2013) speculated that the reasons for the lack of principal diversity might lie in the facts that rural districts traditionally attract fewer applicants than other districts and anticipating a principal vacancy is relatively easy in rural communities.

Superintendents of these districts could begin to groom a known successor in advance of a principal vacancy, making the district less dependent on outside applicants to fill vacant positions and therefore less attentive to the diversity and inclusivity of the applicant pool (Wood et al., 2013). As such, the rural district is more reliant on its professional or social network; if that network is largely homogenous, there will be implicit bias in its recruitment practices.

Explicit Bias

District leaders may prefer to hire principals with whom they share background characteristics, making it more likely that they select a same-race principal from an applicant pool. Hammond et al. (2001) found a perception among aspiring principals in New York State that school district hiring practices exhibited bias based on the applicant's gender and ethnicity. This perception discouraged female applicants of color from pursuing a principal position.

Candidate Interest

Previous research (Tran et al., 2020a) has revealed that a teacher or assistant principal's interest in the principalship is influenced by their perceptions of the job. Principal candidates may prefer to work for a district with same-race representation at the district leadership level or within the principal ranks, and thus be more likely to apply to a race-aligned district or accept a job there if it is offered.

Geographical Limitations

In their review of the literature on rural teaching barriers, Tran et al. (2020b) identified the following challenges to teaching in rural areas: lack of diversity, requirement to teach multiple subjects or grade levels, teaching outside of one's subject, high poverty, limited resources, low pay, the high visibility of teachers in small communities, professional isolation (i.e., lack of professional development and socialization opportunities), less desirable location and fewer amenities (e.g., malls and beaches), as well as inadequate school building facilities without sanitary working and learning conditions (i.e., working plumbing, functional HVAC, ventilation, lighting).

These factors not only deter potential teacher candidates from considering teaching in rural districts, but also can motivate teacher departure in the form of turnover. Of course, many of these influences are relevant for principal staffing as well.

The fact that rural districts are often smaller in size and organization as compared to urban and suburban school districts means that school principals often have to "wear many hats" in rural districts, taking on additional duties such as teaching, bus driving, or janitorial work, which their counterparts in other locales do not share. To exacerbate the situation, the lower enrollment in rural schools often means that those schools do not receive state funding for an assistant principal to support the school leader, making their work even more challenging.

CASE STUDY: MISSING THE MARK
ON PRINCIPAL RECRUITMENT

The district utilized in the case is in the southeastern United States near a large city. Although the district is a suburb of the city, it still has many of the characteristics of a rural area. A suburb like this one, known as an outer-ring suburb, illustrates how suburbanization has resulted in an evolution of residential development in rural areas (Burdick-Will & Logan, 2017). However, these communities are often classified as suburbs by the government despite their historical roots as rural communities. As a result, these schools do not enjoy the same level of economic advantage as schools in the inner suburbs (Burdick-Will & Logan, 2017).

A formal Aspiring Leaders Program acts as a primary tool to assure leadership succession and capacity building in the case district. Components of this program incorporate leadership learning and development opportunities for the district to develop its own leaders through a "grow your own" (GYO) program. It is designed to build the leadership capacity of those who are interested in becoming assistant principals. Participants in the aspiring leader cohort participate in hands-on learning experiences that aim to equip leaders with the skills they need to achieve student success, engage families and the community, develop other leaders, and manage district systems and operations.

To meet the organization's developmental needs, succession planning programs should be constantly revised and monitored (Buckman & Tran, 2022). The case district's GYO leadership program is similar in that it is becoming more formalized and improvement-focused with each cohort's implementation.

Due to the district's homogenous workforce, there are missed opportunities to identify the best talent, especially in response to its diversity needs, since the district relies almost exclusively on internal promotions. The district specifically reported difficulty recruiting educators to match their non-White students, even though the district's workforce is mostly White and prefers internal hiring, likely perpetuating the lack of diversity (Buckman & Tran, 2018).

Additionally, there was backlash from community members from the district's attempt to foster diversity and inclusivity. The anti-diversity response came in the form of threatening phone calls, verbal assaults on the character of school board members, and additional unwarranted scrutiny against the credentials of a newly appointed diversity-centered leader in the district. As a result, the individual who received the position resigned before their actual start date and the position was never filled or readvertised.

As previously mentioned, recruiting for diversity in rural school districts can be difficult based on previous hiring practices, community resources, school dynamics, and cultural issues. Additionally, historical "glass ceilings" and limits to promotion found in traditional rural districts must be addressed to disrupt the traditions of favoritism in promotion toward White male leaders (Cotter et al., 2001).

As mentioned in the case study, to address principal vacancies, some school districts utilize internal promotion and grow their programs as succession-planning mechanisms; however, districts must have a diverse teaching population to develop, nurture, and produce a diverse leadership pool. The absence of diversity in a district's teaching pool will perpetuate a cycle of recruitment and hiring that lacks diversity in school districts that promote primarily from within.

RECOMMENDATIONS FOR DISTRICT-BASED LEADERS TO DIVERSIFY SCHOOL LEADERSHIP

As organizations strive to improve the work culture and climate with a diverse workforce, the practical implications of these recruiting challenges present opportunities to 1) strengthen the connection between district policies and practices, 2) conduct internal and external assessments of organizational climate and culture, 3) align recruiting priorities with execution of strategic plans, and 4) construct practices and policies from equity-minded ideologies that reduce race and/or sex discrimination.

In addition, teachers of color are more likely to stay, be more satisfied, and teach in schools with principals that they racially or ethnically match (Bartanen & Grissom, 2019; Grissom & Keiser, 2011). Consequently, if a school district does not employ any leaders of color and the staffing of such leaders is not an organizational priority (as is the case study scenario), then their staffing challenges with teachers of color will persist. In other words, the relationship between diversifying the teacher body is directly related to the diversity of school leaders, so school employers who are concerned with the former should also be concerned with the latter.

Finally, while traditional human resources management approaches have emphasized the assimilation of new employees to the norms of the organization, modern talent management approaches such as talent-centered education leadership (TCEL) emphasize the intentional design of positive and supportive "employee experiences" to better engage employees (Mazor et al., 2017; Tran, 2020). TCEL, in particular, operates based on seven core principles (Tran & Jenkins, 2022). The principles include the following:

Principle 1: Recognize that employees are the most important asset to the organization, and that educator needs and student needs are not mutually exclusive.

Principle 2: Emphasize inclusive talent management. Talent-centered education leaders create inclusive work environments and understand that the way talent is defined can either marginalize or recognize the diversity of talent and leverage innovation.

Principle 3: Focus on the employee experience (EEX).

Principle 4: Utilize data to inform decision-making, particularly as it relates to designing positive and engaging EEXs.

Principle 5: Empathize with employee needs by authentically and regularly listening to their concerns and feedback, and by providing them with workplace autonomy and flexibility.

Principle 6: Focus on employee engagement as a valued organizational outcome.

Principle 7: Consistently show and demonstrate respect for education employees.

How employers respond to the seven principles, or implement inclusive talent management, can influence the diversity of rural school leadership. For the purposes of this chapter, we focus on Principles 2 and 3, which were most relevant to the case study. To start, the principalship continues to remain majority White (Taie et al., 2019) and leadership expectations continue to remain White, heteronormative, and masculine (Iskander, 2022).

Consequently, traditional exclusionary perspectives on who is considered "leadership material" worthy of being hired into the principalship by school employers, coupled with the common perception that rural spaces are "White spaces" (Edgeworth, 2015), maintains the lack of diversity of rural school leadership both from an employer push perspective (i.e., employer bias results in candidates of color not being hired) and an applicant push perspective (i.e., applicants of color may not be interested in working with the employer).

Rural school employers that operate with the second principle of TCEL in the forefront understand the importance of cultivating inclusive workspaces and pay attention to potential marginalizing effects of organizational stances, practices, and culture. They intentionally work to transform these spaces to become more welcoming.

Rural school employers that espouse the third principle of TCEL understand the importance of empathizing with the needs of their employees, which includes school leaders. This approach is unique in that it puts accountability on the employer for providing supportive and engaging work environments. As Tran and Jenkins (2022) explain,

> TCEL leaders should think about designing an immersive employee experience that considers the employee journey from entry to retirement (Mazor et al.,

2017). Simply bringing employees on board the organization is just the start. By considering the employee experience throughout the entirety of a career, TCEL leaders can increase employee engagement retention for all education employees. (p. 272)

From a diversity perspective, this approach recognizes and acknowledges the potentially different EEXs of leaders from different demographic backgrounds and seeks to create a work setting that welcomes all to bring their authentic selves to work. Doing this can not only attract but retain leaders across the spectrum of diversity.

CONCLUSION

Increasing the racial/ethnic diversity of the principalship is an imperative since school districts are struggling with diversifying their declining teacher workforces. Currently, a need exists to increase the recruitment and retention efforts for principals of color in geographically remote areas of the United States. Intentional recruitment of principals of color can positively impact the experiences of students of color by establishing a school improvement agenda and creating safe and supportive teaching and learning environments.

Diverse principals also influence the quality and performance of instructional staff and can be a determining factor in teachers' decisions to accept employment or remain in a school. Furthermore, addressing the administrative, organizational, financial, professional, and personal incentives and disincentives to becoming a principal can expand the applicant pool and its diversity. Incorporating the recommended strategies will pay future dividends in both the number and quality of those who are willing to meet the challenges of the principal position in rural areas of the United States.

REFERENCES

Achinstein, B., Ogawa, R. T., Sexton, D., & Freitas, C. (2010). Retaining teachers of color: A pressing problem and a potential strategy for "hard-to-staff" schools. *Review of Educational Research, 80*(1), 71–107. https://doi.org/10.3102/0034654309355994

Amos, Y. T. (2016). Voices of teacher candidates of color on White race evasion: "I worried about my safety!" *International Journal of Qualitative Studies in Education, 29*(8), 1002–1015. https://doi.org/10.1080/09518398.2016.1174900

Bartanen, B., & Grissom, J. (2019). *School principal race and the hiring and retention of racially diverse teachers* (EdWorkingPaper No.19–59). Annenberg Institute at Brown University. http://edworkingpapers.com/ai19-59

Bartanen, B., & Grissom, J. (2021). School principal race, teacher racial diversity, and student achievement. *Journal of Human Resources*, 0218–9328R2. https://doi.org/10.3368/jhr.58.4.0218–9328R2

Bristol. T. J. (2015). Teaching boys: Towards a theory of gender-relevant pedagogy. *Gender and Education*, *27*(1), 53–68.

Bristol, T. J. (2018). To be alone or in a group: An exploration into how the school-based experiences differ for Black male teachers across one urban school district. *Urban Education*, *53*(3), 334–354.

Bristol, T. J., & Martin-Fernandez, J. (2019). The added value of Latinx and Black teachers for Latinx and Black students: Implications for policy. *Policy Insights from the Behavioral and Brain Sciences*, *6*(2), 147–153.

Buckman, D., & Tran, H. (2018). Internal and external elementary principal hiring and minimal student achievement: A 5-year cohort model. *International Journal of Educational Leadership Preparation*, *13*(1), 1–17.

Buckman, D., & Tran, H. (2022). Scholarship versus practice: Best succession planning practices from scholarship as compared with practices employed by a large outer-ring suburban school district in the field. In L. L. Sabina (Ed.). *School administrator succession planning: Identifying high-impact practices, programs, and frameworks in P–12 schools* (pp. 65–88). Information Age Publishing.

Burdick-Will, J., & Logan, J. R. (2017). Schools at the rural-urban boundary: Blurring the divide? *The ANNALS of the American Academy of Political and Social Science*, *672*(1), 185–201.

Carter Andrews, D. J., Castro, E., Cho, C. L., Petchauer, E., Richmond, G., & Floden, R. (2019). Changing the narrative on diversifying the teaching workforce: A look at historical and contemporary factors that inform recruitment and retention of teachers of color. *Journal of Teacher Education*, *70*(1), 6–12. https://doi.org/10.1177/0022487118812418

Carver-Thomas, D. (2018). *Diversifying the teaching profession: How to recruit and retain teachers of color*. Learning Policy Institute. https://doi.org/10.54300/559.310

Castro, A.J., Germain, E., & Gooden, M.A. (2018). *Increasing diversity in K–12 school leadership*. Policy Brief No. 2018–3. University Council for Educational Administration.

Cotter, D. A., Hermsen, J. M., Ovadia, S., & Vanneman, R. (2001). The glass ceiling effect. *Social Forces*, *80*(2), 655–668.

Cruzeiro, P. A., & Boone, M. (2009). Rural and small school principal candidate: Perspectives of hiring superintendents. *The Rural Educator*, *31*(1), 1–9.

Doyle, D., & Locke, G. (2014). *Lacking leaders: The challenges of principal recruitment, selection, and placement*. Thomas B. Fordham Institute. https://fordhaminstitute.org/national/research/lacking-leaders-challenges-principal-recruitment-selection-and-placement

Easton-Brooks, D., Lewis, C. W., & Zhang, Y. (2009). Ethnic matching: The influence of African American teachers on the reading scores of African American students. *The Journal of Urban Education & Practice*, *3*(1), 235–243.

Edgeworth, K. (2015). Black bodies, White rural spaces: Disturbing practices of unbelonging for "refugee" students. *Critical Studies in Education*, *56*(3), 351–365.

Frankenberg, E., & Orfield, G. (2012). *The resegregation of suburban schools: A hidden crisis in American education*. Harvard Education Press.

Gershenson, S., Hart, C. M. D., Lindsay, C. A., & Papageorge, N. W. (2017). *The long-run impacts of same-race teachers* (Discussion Paper No. 10630). IZA Institute of Labor Economics. https://docs.iza.org/dp10630.pdf

Gist, C. (2014). The culturally responsive teacher educator. *The Teacher Educator, 49*, 265–283.

Goings, R. B., & Bianco, M. (2016). It's hard to be who you don't see: An exploration of Black male high school students' perspectives on becoming teachers. *The Urban Review, 48*, 628–646.

Grissom, J. A., & Keiser, L. R. (2011). A supervisor like me: Race, representation, and the satisfaction and turnover decisions of public sector employees. *Journal of Policy Analysis and Management, 30*(3), 557–580.

Grissom, J. A., & Redding, C. (2016). Discretion and disproportionality: Explaining the underrepresentation of high-achieving students of color in gifted programs. *AERA Online, 2*(1), 1–15. https://doi.org/10.1177/2332858415622175

Hammond, J., Muffs, M., & Sciascia, S. (2001). The leadership crisis: Is it for real? *Principal, 81*(2), pp. 28–29, 31–32.

Healy, L. (2016). *K–12 school districts work to improve inclusion through teacher training*. INSIGHT into Diversity. https://www.insightintodiversity.com/k-12-school-districts-work-to-improve-inclusion-through-teacher-training/

Ingersoll, R. M., May, H., & Collins, G. (2017). *Minority teacher recruitment, employment, and retention: 1987 to 2013*. Learning Policy Institute. https://repository.upenn.edu/gse_pubs/496

Ingersoll, R., Merrill, L., & May, H. (2014). *What are the effects of teacher education and preparation on beginning teacher attrition?* (Report No. RR-82). Consortium for Policy Research in Education, University of Pennsylvania. https://www.cpre.org/sites/default/files/researchreport/2018_prepeffects2014.pdf

Iskander, L. (2022). "I assumed it was a much safer place than it really is": Nonbinary educators' strategies for finding school jobs. *Journal of Education Human Resources, 40*(1), 114–134. https://doi.org/10.3138/jehr-2021-0009

Lee, S. W., & Mao, X. (2020). Recruitment and selection of principals: A systematic review. *Educational Management Administration & Leadership, 51*(1), 6–29. https://doi.org/10.1177/1741143220969694

Mahatmya, D., Grooms, A. A., Young Kim, J., McGinnis, D., & Johnson, E. (2022). Burnout and race-related stress among BIPOC women K–12 educators. *Journal of Education Human Resources, 40*(1), 58–89.

Mazor, A. H., Zucker, J., Sivak, M., Coombes, R., & Van Durme, Y. (2017). *Reimagine and craft the employee experience: Design thinking in action*. Deloitte Development LLC. https://www2.deloitte.com/us/en/pages/human-capital/articles/reimagine-and-craft-the-employee-experience.html

National Center for Education Statistics (NCES). (2019a). Table 212.15: Percentage distribution of principals in public elementary and secondary schools, by school locale and selected characteristics: 2017–18. Institute of Education Sciences, U.S.

Department of Education. https://nces.ed.gov/programs/digest/d19/tables/dt19_212.15.asp

National Center for Education Statistics (NCES). (2019b). Table 209.26: Percentage distribution of teachers in public elementary and secondary schools, by school locale and selected teacher characteristics: 2017–18. Institute of Education Sciences, U.S. Department of Education. https://nces.ed.gov/programs/digest/d19/tables/dt19_209.26.asp

Nzau, S., Busette, C., Reeves, R. V., & Frimpong, K. (2021). *Social networks and economic mobility: What the findings reveal*. Brookings Institute. https://www.brookings.edu/blog/how-we-rise/2021/03/09/social-networks-and-economic-mobility-what-the-findings-reveal/

Partelow, L., Spong, A., Brown, C., & Johnson, S. (2017). *America needs more teachers of color and a more selective teaching profession*. Center for American Progress. https://www.americanprogress.org/issues/education-k-12/reports/2017/09/14/437667/america-needs-teachers-color-selective-teaching-profession/

Putman, H., Hansen, M., Walsh, K., & Quintero, D. (2016). *High hopes and harsh realities: The real challenges to building a diverse teacher workforce*. Brookings Institution. https://www.brookings.edu/research/high-hopes-and-harsh-realities-the-real-challenges-to-building-a-diverse-teacher-workforce/

Sleeter, C. E. (2001). Preparing teachers for culturally diverse schools: Research and the overwhelming presence of Whiteness. *Journal of Teacher Education*, 52(2), 94–106.

Taie, S., Goldring, R., & Spiegelman, M. (2019). *Characteristics of public and private elementary and secondary school principals in the United States: Results from the 2017–18 National Teacher and Principal Survey* (Report No. 2019-141). National Center for Education Statistics, U.S. Department of Education.

Tran, H. (2020). Revolutionizing school HR strategies and practices to reflect talent centered education leadership. *Leadership and Policy in Schools*, 21(2), 1–15. https://doi.org/10.1080/15700763.2020.1757725

Tran, H., & Jenkins, Z. (2022). Embracing the future of education work with talent centered education leadership. *Journal of Education Human Resources*, 40(2), 266–276. https://doi.org/10.3138/jehr-2021-0051

Tran, H., Buckman, D., & Johnson, A. (2020a). Using the hiring process to improve the cultural responsiveness of schools. *Journal of Cases in Education Leadership*, 23(2), 70–84. https://doi.org/10.1177/1555458920904767

Tran, H., Hardie, S., Gause, S., Moyi, P., & Ylimaki, R. (2020b). Leveraging the perspectives of rural educators to develop realistic job previews for rural teacher recruitment and retention. *The Rural Educator*, 41(2), 31–46. https://doi.org/10.35608/ruraled.v41i2.866

Wood, J. N., Finch, K., & Mirecki, R. M. (2013). If we get you, how can we keep you? Problems with recruiting and retaining rural administrators. *The Rural Educator*, 34(2). https://doi.org/10.35608/ruraled.v34i2.399

Chapter 6

Retaining Principals
What Works Best?

Belinda Gimbert and Dustin W. Miller,
The Ohio State University

Policymakers and educators have known for many years that effective school leadership is associated with better outcomes for students and school communities (Adams & Muthiah, 2020; Day et al., 2016; Heffernan, 2021; Leithwood et al., 2020). Longevity of an effective principal's tenure can nurture school improvement, strengthen classroom instruction, engage school communities, and retain staff—all linchpins for P–12 students' academic and social growth. This is old, yet good, news that principals do matter! And beyond this, steady and tenacious leadership matters!

Competent and caring leaders of elementary and secondary schools undergird educators' efforts to promote equitable learning opportunities that advance academic performance for every student (Bartanen et al., 2019; Snodgrass Rangel, 2018; Yan, 2020). In reaction to national conversations referencing the "constant, expensive churn of experienced principals," the public expects responses to the questions, What is known about patterns of principal attrition? and How can effective principals be retained to positively impact their school's working and learning conditions? Understanding why a principal chooses to stay in the profession can help policymakers and district leaders improve conditions and entice principals to remain throughout their careers.

While individual characteristics such as gender, age, minority status, experience, and school background variables such as location, grade level, size, poverty status, and student demographics can disrupt principal longevity, the deleterious impact of principal attrition accelerates a downturn in student achievement (Beckett, 2021; Tran & Buckman, 2017).

Furthermore, as school systems face the consequences of an unprecedented public health crisis due to COVID-19, such as a rising exodus of educators from the profession, the need for principals to stay should raise even more urgent attention from schools, districts, and state departments of education.

Guided by a current and comprehensive understanding of the consequences of local principal attrition and mobility patterns on their students (and families), district leaders can systemically initiate and sustain targeted supports for retaining effective principals at their schools, as well as for those intentionally reassigned to a new school (Stone-Johnson & Weiner, 2020). Of course, not all school leaders should be retained. In such cases, action steps should be taken to relieve principals of their professional duties and obligations if they are unable to lead in a learning context that meets their students' academic outcomes (Levin et al., 2019).

In this chapter, we discuss what is known about factors that impact P–12 principal retention, including school, school district, and local education agency characteristics such as levels of resources, competitive salaries, working conditions, and accountability measures (which may also influence principals' longevity of tenure and job satisfaction). Initially, we interrogated our own researcher knowledge, asking ourselves the following questions:

- What do we know about principal retention in general? Stories of principals who leave their career foretell unsought outcomes for students, educators, and the public.
- What do we know about how to improve principal retention in higher-turnover contexts? Quite a lot! What are educators doing with what is known?
- Does principal retention differ across school districts, local educational agencies, and schools within districts? Yes, it varies. Why?
- Does principal retention vary depending on principalship experience, and do retention rates diverge from one-year principal retention to more than three-year retention? Yes, but why?
- Does principal retention depend on grade span, student race/ethnicity, poverty level, and student academic performance? Yes to all! Why?

Next, and in response to our mutual reflection, we applied a literature synthesis to capture a collective understanding of what is known from scholarly studies of principal retention from over the last fifteen years. The following questions guided this search:

- What is the goal of policymakers and education leaders of retaining principals?
- What are the expanded outcomes for all school stakeholders of retaining principals?
- What are the local impacts of principal turnover and, conversely, principal retention on the school and school community?
- Which principals are more likely to stay in their jobs?
- Why do principals leave their jobs?
- What keeps principals in their jobs?

An extensive literature search uncovered six effective evidenced-based practices for retaining principals, which are named and discussed in the next section. Influential factors, as well as intended and unintended outcomes, are evinced to inform policymakers and practitioners' understandings of what works most effectively to bolster principal retention. Understudied areas needing additional research emerged, notably differences in P–12 principals' experiences of leading for learning in high- versus low-poverty schools (Levin et al., 2020; Yan, 2020) and the implications of those differences for leadership development and principal retention.

We advocate actions by states and local systems to invest in more informed legislative and programmatic responses to retain principals. After all, reducing principal attrition by attending to its root causes is crucial to student academic success and to educational organizations' fiscal survival, since turnover of school leaders is one of the costliest challenges facing American public schools (Bartanen et al., 2019; Beckett, 2021; Hom et al., 2017; Levin et al., 2020; Tran et al., 2018).

WHY DO PRINCIPALS STAY, MOVE, OR LEAVE?

The extant scholarship is replete with studies documenting factors at the school and district levels that influence how and why principals pursue career transitions. Whether they elect to stay, move, or leave the profession, principals are influenced, among other dynamics, by their personal characteristics, workplace conditions, emotional aspects of their labor, and moral reactions to teaching and learning.

We interpret six evidenced-based practices from our literature synthesis that undergird principal stability, which policymakers and practitioners can implement to sustain "sure-footed" leaders (i.e., principals who focus on improving instruction for all students and who stay the course within their school community).

Principals should encounter the following practices to increase the likelihood that they will stay in the profession:

1. Receive organizational and personalized supports related to workplace conditions, stable and adequate compensation, and decision-making authority (including district-level policies).
2. Have a sense of belonging and self-efficacy to enhance job satisfaction and the longevity of effective leadership.
3. Foster collegial relationships.
4. Co-lead with the school community, aligning leader, school, and community visions and gaining parent input.
5. Engage in succession planning.
6. Experience high-quality and developmentally appropriate professional learning (including pre-service and induction learning opportunities), and build strong networks.

Practice One: Receive Organizational and Personalized Supports

Workplace Conditions

From anecdotal stories alone, few would disagree that the present-day life of a principal is daunting. Goldring and Taie (2014) predicted a principal's time commitment exceeds sixty hours per week. Other researchers portray the daily work of a contemporary principal as more demanding and complex than prospective school leaders anticipate (Elomaa et al. 2021; Grissom et al., 2015). Principals experience more occupational stress than the general population, which researchers claim is caused by intense workloads and difficulties in interpersonal relationships (Mahfouz, 2020).

Principals assume an abundance of responsibilities that include supervising teachers, disciplining students, involving parents, managing facilities and budgets, distributing resources, leading faculty meetings, establishing technology regulations, and caring for students and staff (Beausaert et al., 2016; Darmody & Smyth, 2016). Such tasks render time a scarce commodity that principals must allocate among competing job demands (Grissom et al., 2015). The number of work hours may induce job-related stress that manifests as burnout and increases the risk of turnover (Mahfouz, 2020; Tintore et al., 2020).

Stable and Adequate Compensation

Past findings suggest a principal's satisfaction with their salary may be a potential determinant in a decision to leave or stay at a school. For instance,

Baker er al. (2010) reported that the higher a principal's remuneration relative to peers (other principals within the same district or principals in other school districts), the less likely the school leader is to leave.

Tran and Buckman (2017) explored how building leaders feel about their salary in relation to remaining in the principalship and suggested that high school principals' pay satisfaction is influenced by salaries of peers and is positively correlated with principals' intentions to stay in leadership roles. Principals who were more satisfied with their pay were more likely to want to stay in the position of principal.

Other researchers claim compensation for school leaders in US school districts is inadequate to improve principal retention. Some note that a principal's pay is so compressed when compared to teacher salaries in urban centers that it is no surprise educators choose not to assume the expanded workload of a principal (Beckett, 2021; Yan, 2020). It is little wonder that attracting individuals to the principalship with its extra demands continues to propagate a widely accepted perception that financial incentives do not justify the extended and intensified work commitment expected of school leaders.

Decision-Making Authority

Notably, Tekleselassie and Villarreal (2011) reported that positive conditions pertaining to the emotional aspects of the principal's work and the perceived degree of influence over the people and policies of the school combined to increase the likelihood of the principal's retention. This was despite other school and district characteristics.

Principals in their study stated that their authority to make budget, hiring, and curricula decisions and to direct evaluation processes were nonnegotiable aspects of their authority. Further, principals with authority to make decisions related to teacher dismissal for poor performance are more likely to consider staying in the profession (Levin et al., 2020).

From a wider perspective, supportive union policies may leverage principals' career-related decisions and incentivize them to stay because negotiated regulations monitor and improve their salaries (Han, 2020). Principals may feel more secure if their tenure is protected, thereby relieving the pressure of dismissal at will, and thus they may be more committed to carrying out their professional responsibilities (Choi & Park, 2020). Additionally, when principals feel empowered by district and teacher union policies that support what they know is in the best interest of students and their families, then they are more likely to stay in key leadership roles (Levin et al, 2020).

Scholars indicate that conditions influencing intention to leave may not necessarily predict intention to move, suggesting that different forms of exit behaviors require different policy tools to address them. Boyce and

Bowers (2016) identified two types of departing principals: "satisfied leavers" incentivized by promotion opportunities and/or better hiring packages, and "disaffected leavers," dispirited by low levels of efficacy and adverse school climate.

Tekleselassie and Choi (2021) offer a unique perspective about how district-level policies that target improved working conditions for teachers may aid principal stability—that is, the influence of teacher retention on principal retention is worth considering. School districts with professional enticements, such as a career ladder with national board certification and/or financial incentives that attract teachers to work in less desirable locations, appear to lessen principal movement.

The question to ask here is how incentives may increase teachers' morale and job satisfaction and influence them to stay at the same school, which may alleviate pressure on principals to constantly rehire staff. Regrettably, US school districts typically do not have policies with similar incentives for principals. Rather, increasing work obligations without incentives can induce work-related stress and discourage a principal from staying. Conversely, realistic expectations and support to reduce intolerable challenges may coalesce to create job security and satisfaction, encouraging career longevity.

Practice Two: Have a Sense of Belonging and Self-Efficacy

Recent global attention on the effects of expanding principal workloads amplified the negative consequences that impact principal retention (Beausaert et al., 2016; Liu & Bellibas, 2018). The intensifying nature of a school leader's job today reflects images of overwork and stress, which influence health, well-being, and longevity in the role. Principals face a high risk of burnout due to serious pressure to perform and ensure that others perform, which is directly connected to the likelihood of quitting (Beausaert et al., 2016; Heffernan, 2021).

Principals who serve long tenures are most likely the *right* leaders in the *right* positions (Fink, 2010). To mitigate stress and burnout and increase the likelihood of withstanding the challenges inherent in the role, a principal must "fit" with the contextual nuances of a place, such as a highly marginalized community with vulnerable students and families, or a school district seeking to diversify its leadership workforce in a challenging setting, or a more resourced community with stable and experienced leadership.

However, a "good fit" does not eliminate all stress and pressure, since principals are entrenched in their communities (Beausaert et al., 2016; Choi & Park, 2020) and "likely to feel and experience the stresses of their school surrounds more viscerally" (Heffernan, 2021, p. 3).

Increased job satisfaction may lengthen a school leader's tenure and influence departure intentions, thereby potentially alleviating risk of attrition (Postma & Babo, 2019). School leaders who have left the profession blame job dissatisfaction for their choice. Extrinsic factors such as arduous workload, nebulous role definition, poor peer relationships, and inequitable comparative salary contribute to a decision to leave (Chang et al., 2015; Darmody & Smyth, 2016).

In addition, lower measures of intrinsic attributes such as "a perceived level of satisfaction with the district and school, degree of enthusiasm in their job, assessment of faculty satisfaction in their job, and perceived energy level to continue work as principals" are correlated with school leaders' departure (Tekleselassie & Choi, 2021, p. 1145).

Dispositional or affective factors such as self-esteem, emotional stability, and self-efficacy influence a principal's job satisfaction (Mahfouz, 2020), which strengthens as "belief in their own abilities to succeed in the job increases" (Postma & Babo, 2019, p. 84). Postma and Babo also found that principals' reported self-efficacy in management was strongly linked to job satisfaction. However, another study of the job satisfaction of highly educated professionals classified by gender and race found that Black principals are less satisfied than White principals (Hersch & Xiao, 2015).

For educators, work-life boundaries tend to blur (Shah et al., 2010). In the case of principals, personal lives weigh heavily on career trajectory decisions. When professional life impinges on personal relationships, work-family conflict may ensue, with serious negative consequences related to decisions to leave. A principal's sense of moral purpose may trump other local conditions such as the impact on a principal's family associated with working and living in a small school community.

Principals state a desire to return to a location closer to "home," near family, friends, and even sometimes schools where they were educated. The lure of positive personal networks and past experiences should not be ignored. Benefits and drawbacks of these contextual factors continue to overtly influence career decisions.

This highlights the importance of local strategy and policies (Wilkerson & Wilson, 2017) that enable a principal to see the long-term impacts of their work and gauge their progress in leading "cultural shifts in the school and community" (Heffernan, 2021, p. 8). In addition, a sense of achievement from their intense effort to establish themselves may motivate principals to stay in their current positions (Wang et al., 2018).

Practice Three: Foster Collegial Relationships

Unquestionably, principal–teacher relationships inform a school leader's decision to move or leave the profession (Snodgrass Rangel, 2018; Stone-Johnson & Weiner, 2020). Conversely, teachers cite principal advocacy and professional support as important influences on their decision to stay in a school or in the educational field (Levin et al., 2019).

School leaders should be keenly aware that their interpersonal skills that demonstrate care, character, and integrity affect the strength of the trust they earn. Relatedly, teacher and staff cynicism and resistance to change decrease with longevity of effective leadership (Northfield, 2014; Lee 2015).

District supervisors who provide professional support for principals are described as accessible and visible. Principals portray their immediate supervisor as a critical ally during informal visits, and as an evaluative advocate in more formal situations. Principals who intend to stay illustrated a relationship with their supervisors as safe, challenging, and essential for their tenure (Cieminski, 2018; Bartanen et al., 2019).

Sensing a supervisor's commitment to protecting them and growing their leadership competencies, principals seem surer of their decision to remain. Despite this, scholars note a lack of formalized policies and intentional practices for managing the workload of principals, providing personalized support for new and experienced administrators, or developing skills of district leaders to induct and mentor principals, which are all specifically aimed at retaining effective building leaders or identifying potential leaders (Levin et al., 2020).

When principals adopt distributed or shared leadership, assistant principals can also aspects of building leadership, including how to model evidenced-based instructional practices and assess their teachers' daily pedagogical praxis. With this teamwork approach, principals feel empowered to advocate for more challenging student learning outcomes, which then fuels their commitment to professional learning communities (Parylo & Zepeda, 2015).

Opportunities emerge for potential principal candidates when principals create roles for teacher leaders such as "committee leader, grade level or department chairperson, member of district-level and building level committees, or summer school principal" (Cieminski, 2018, p. 33). Often principals select master teachers to perform work as quasi-administrators, such as instructional coaches or teachers on special assignment.

In some instances, principals purposefully structure these learning experiences to assess an individual's leadership potential for future principal preparation. It would seem when a principal intentionally engages a peer in this way, each can learn from their background experiences and grow a synergistic relationship that nurtures shared leadership through collective decision-making.

Practice Four: Co-Lead with the School Community

In general, principals struggle with establishing and maintaining effective communication pathways among school stakeholders and communities, which impacts how they feel about their leadership (Beckett, 2021). Within a conceptual framework of leading in the midst of diversity, principals who feel empowered to express their ideals of an inclusive learning community model a vision of leadership that actively encourages others to participate. Involving parents relates to parent satisfaction, student engagement and persistence, and student social competence (Tekleselassie & Choi, 2021).

While little is known about the impact of parental involvement on principals' intention to stay, Blaik Hourani and Stringer (2015) suggest that how parents participate may reflect on a school's climate and consequently impact principal retention. Growing productive partnerships, caring for the well-being of students and families, and weaving cultural norms into the fabric of a school's mission and vision require extensive knowledge about how best to involve parents in supporting their school.

When principals consider parents' assets and interactions with them are embraced, they are more likely to stay. When principals view parents as liabilities who hamper a principal's interactions with teachers and students, they are more likely to leave. In summary, a school leader's competency for leading an inclusive school community relates to the skill of "encouraging participation in collective cultures of learning" (Blaik Hourani & Stringer, 2015, p. 314) and communicating effectively with all stakeholders.

A principal can strategically unite community stakeholders and resources as well as other local agencies to design and guide mutually beneficial partnerships for the well-being of students and their families. In doing so, a principal's credibility grows as a result of their local advocacy.

Practice Five: Engage in Succession Planning

Despite perceived leadership shortages and high turnover rates of school leaders, little attention has been given to succession planning for P–12 principals by states, school districts, or practitioners. For the purposes of this chapter, we explain principal succession "as a leadership transition process produced by the departure of a principal and the arrival of another" (Aravena, 2022, p. 356).

Researchers describe succession planning (Bush, 2022; Cieminski, 2018) as an effort by more experienced district leaders to grow leadership quality for school improvement. The goal is to deliver targeted support for individuals moving into principal positions while cultivating a mentoring relationship with their more experienced peers. In concert with researchers (Fusarelli et al., 2018), we promote succession planning as a systemic practice that ties together processes to recruit and retain P–12 school leaders, in our case principals.

Although research on succession planning may be thin (Aravena, 2022), leadership succession is a disruptive force (positive or negative) to the social dynamics within a school and its community (Snodgrass Rangel, 2018). Potential rapid and repeated threats to principal transition may be negated if conditions are based on sound decision-making and planning (Fink, 2010; Lee, 2015). Therefore, how can succession planning contribute to strengthening and stabilizing principal leadership?

We propose that the following key action steps be embedded into succession planning to stabilize principal movement:

1. Address the negative and target the positive impacts of change associated with school leadership succession (Fink, 2010) while simultaneously building on the strengths of incoming and current principals (Cocklin & Wilkinson, 2011).
2. Develop awareness and understanding about how principal succession impacts teacher morale (Cieminski, 2018).
3. Engage in work-shadowing as a process for facilitating leadership succession (Simkins et al., 2009).
4. In the absence of a formal succession plan, grow teacher leader programs and identify local talent for future school leader positions (Anthony et al., 2019).
5. Build trust with staff as part of early-phase school leadership during principal succession (Northfield, 2014).
6. Develop principal competencies through the lens of an organizational socialization theory (Zepeda et al., 2012).

At its core, a plan for leader transition is social. While collegial interaction is relevant to understanding how principals socialize and build their own role identity, mentoring and coaching appear crucial in a successful principal succession plan. Scholars emphasize the positive contribution of mentoring to principal retention (Bush, 2022; Lee, 2015; Zepeda et al., 2012). Adopting a mentoring approach can support the learning needs of prospective and new principals and bolster the tenure of more experienced leaders (James-Ward, 2013).

Practice Six: Experience High-Quality and Developmentally Appropriate Professional Learning

Recent evidence supports Lewis and Murphy's (2008) earlier claim that skilled school leaders create and sustain more equitable learning conditions for all students (Beckett, 2021; Blaik Hourani & Stringer, 2015; Levin et al., 2019) and better working environments and communication among teachers and staff (Beckett, 2021). Localized rates of principal retention increase when school leaders experience meaningful and sustained learning opportunities that include ongoing coaching and specialized training beyond mentoring within a succession plan for new principals (Cieminski, 2018; James-Ward, 2013).

For example, drawing on their site-specific concerns about teacher effectiveness and student learning issues, principals call for professional support from experienced peers who present as go-to colleagues with hands-on experience. To understand their responsibilities, principals seek to learn the parameters of the job from mentors (Bush, 2022).

In addition, principals may look to other resources such as a job aide or district policy, including a documented process to follow that accommodates changing expectations for professional performance (Blaik Hourani & Stringer, 2015; Levin et al., 2020). Often these resources do not exist or are not up-to-date (Hom et al., 2017).

Principals voice a need for professional direction around writing and changing policies to suit their schools' needs in terms of health and safety, communicating with parents, technology accessibility and security, and handling facilities, among other managerial functions (Heffernan, 2021). Principals call for tailored attention to their requests to meet school demands that are particular to their individual sites. Principals are typically exposed to generalized professional development, which is not helpful for advancing their context-specific professional competencies and school needs (James-Ward, 2013).

For example, school district leaders can offer differentiated professional development opportunities for principals (Levin et al., 2020) while providing substitute school leaders in their absence (Parylo & Zepeda, 2015). Implementing a process that distributes or shares leadership responsibilities among a team of building leaders has been shown to retain principals and positively impact student learning and organizational outcomes (Leithwood et al., 2020).

PROMISING PRACTICES FOR INCREASING PRINCIPAL RETENTION

Since retaining principals matters to students, educators, school districts, policymakers, and the public, addressing the supply of leaders using evidenced-based best practices appears relatively uncomplicated. Principals want access to organizational and personalized support. They need a sense of belonging, and desire to feel good about their work as leaders and their relationships with staff.

Compassion for others and giving back to the community are typical trademarks of principals' daily practice. They look to others for guidance and listen to their school community. Principals who lead for longevity ask for, value, and act on input. They deserve a fair salary for the extraordinary hours they keep, and perhaps tangible rewards such as a fiscal bonus that acknowledges their competency and tenure as a valued employee. So, why does an outcome of stabilizing a strong leadership workforce seem so unattainable at present?

Our analysis of available research reinforces how incredibly disruptive principal turnover is to maintaining a healthy school climate and learning gains, particularly for under-resourced students who must rely on education for future career opportunities. We are reminded of the financial constraints placed on schools and school districts when one US school in every five replaces its principal each year (Bartanen et al., 2019; Goldring & Taie, 2014).

Our literature synthesis also reveals how evidence-based retention practices can successfully support a strong and stable principal workforce that builds trust within the school community, inspires teaching professionals to stay in teaching, and focuses on equitable instruction for every student. Every state and school district is looking for a panacea for retaining effective school leaders and making school leadership a more attractive career choice, but many factors contribute to principal retention. A first step they can engage in is overhauling their principal preparation programs.

Another solution rests in the balance between accountability measures; job security; and demanding schedules at one end and the need for support of staff, students, and their families; tenure and career progression; and time for professional learning at the other end. Policymakers and practitioners need to know more about the characteristics of the school leaders who choose to stay in the profession. Why do they stay in their contexts of teaching and learning? We encourage researchers to attend to these questions to inform both national dialogue and local actions regarding how to retain and sustain school leaders.

CONCLUSION

The challenges of principal retention are not insurmountable. We can act on strategies conducive to better workplace conditions that influence school leaders' job satisfaction and affective reactions, which are both tied to stress and workload concerns. We can advocate for district policies that positively impact principals' tenure security, permit decision-making authority, and extend communication within the school community. It may be stating the obvious, but it is worth reiterating: We seek to retain effective principals who inspire the best possible education outcomes for the school, its students and staff, and its community.

We wish to elevate effective principals who lead learning with commitment and courage, who are unafraid to do things differently. Principals should be rewarded with resources to amplify their voice and exemplify their leadership. School leaders need safe spaces to grow their competencies in ways that positively impact all who work and learn under their care.

Those who lead the leaders need to proactively reduce principals' work pressures and personal stress by rewarding them with job security and opportunities for high-quality mentoring with their experienced peers. In addition to helping the individual principal develop self-efficacy and competence, we will, more importantly, build better learning environments in schools where teachers and students are constantly improving.

REFERENCES

Adams, D., & Muthiah, V. (2020). School principals and 21st century leadership challenges: A systematic review. *Journal of Nusantara Studies, 5*(1), 189–210.

Anthony, A. B., Gimbert, B., Luke. J. B., & Hurt, M. H. (2019). Distributed leadership in context: Teacher leaders' contributions to novice teacher induction. *Journal of School Leadership, 29*(1), 53–83.

Aravena, F. (2022). Principal succession in schools: A literature review (2003–2019). *Educational Management Administration & Leadership, 50*(3), 354–370.

Baker, B., Punswick, E., & Belt, C. (2010) School leadership stability, principal moves, and departures: Evidence from Missouri. *Education Administration Quarterly, 46*(4), 523–557.

Bartanen, B., Grissom, J. A., & Rogers, L. K. (2019). The impacts of principal turnover. *Educational Evaluation and Policy Analysis, 41*(3), 350–374.

Beausaert, S., Froehlich, S., Devos, C., & Riley, P. (2016). Effects of support on stress and burnout in school principals. *Educational Research, 58*(4), 347–365.

Beckett, L. (2021). Predictors of urban principal turnover. *Urban Education, 56*(10), 1695–1718.

Blaik Hourani, R., & Stringer, P. (2015). Professional development: Perceptions of benefits for principals. *International Journal of Leadership in Education, 18*(3), 305–339.

Boyce, J., & Bowers, A. J. (2016). Principal turnover: Are there different types of principals who move from or leave their schools? A latent class analysis of the 2007–2008 Schools and Staffing Survey and the 2008–2009 Principal Follow-Up Survey. *Leadership and Policy in Schools, 15*, 237–272.

Bush, T. (2022). Succession planning for school principals: System control or leader agency? *Educational Management Administration & Leadership, 50*(3), 351–353.

Chang, Y., Leach, N., & Anderman, E. (2015). The role of perceived autonomy support in principals' affective organizational commitment and job satisfaction. *Social Psychology of Education, 18*(2), 315–336.

Choi, Y., & Park, N. K. (2020), Examining the pull, the push, and their simultaneous effects on managerial turnover. *Management Decision, 58*(12), 2639–2654.

Cieminski, A. (2018). Practices that support leadership succession and principal retention. *ICPEL Education Leadership Review, 19*(1), 21–40.

Cocklin, B., & Wilkinson, J. (2011). A case study of leadership transition: Continuity and change. *Educational Management Administration & Leadership, 39*(6), 661–675.

Darmody, M., & Smyth, E. (2016). Primary school principals' job satisfaction and occupational stress. *International Journal of Educational Management, 30*(1), 115–128.

Day, C., Gu, Q., & Sammos, P. (2016). The impact of leadership on student outcomes: How successful school leaders use transformational and instructional strategies to make a difference. *Educational Administration Quarterly, 52*, 221–258.

Elomaa, M., Eskelä-Haapanen, S., Pakarinen, E., Halttunen, L., & Lerkkanen, M. (2021). Work-related stress of elementary school principals in Finland: Coping strategies and support. *Educational Management Administration & Leadership*, 1–21. https://doi.org/10.1177/17411432211010317

Fink, D. (2010). *The succession challenge: Building and sustaining leadership capacity through succession management*. SAGE Publications.

Fusarelli, B. C., Fusarelli, L. D., & Riddick, F. (2018) Planning for the future: Leadership development and succession planning education. *Journal of Research on Leadership Education, 13*(3), 286–313.

Goldring, R., & Taie, S. (2014). *Principal attrition and mobility: Results from the 2012–13 Principal Follow-Up Survey* (Report No. 2014–064REV). National Center for Education Statistics, U.S. Department of Education. https://nces.ed.gov/pubs2014/2014064rev.pdf

Grissom, J. A., Loeb, S., & Mitani, H. (2015). Principal time management skills: Explaining patterns in principals' time use, job stress, and perceived effectiveness. *Journal of Educational Administration, 53*(6), 773–793.

Han, E. S. (2020). The myth of unions' overprotection of bad teachers: Evidence from the district–teacher matched data on teacher turnover. *Industrial Relations: A Journal of Economy and Society, 59*(2), 316–352.

Heffernan, A. (2021). Retaining Australia's school leaders in "challenging" contexts: The importance of personal relationships in principal turnover decisions. *International Journal of Educational Research, 105*, 101716. http://doi.org/10.1016/J.IJER.2020.10171610.1016/J.IJER.2020.101716

Hersch, J. & Xiao, J. (2016). Sex, race and job satisfaction among highly educated workers. *Southern Economic Journal, 83(1), 1–24.*

Hom, P. W., Lee, T., Shaw, J., & Hausknecht, J. (2017). One hundred years of employee turnover theory and research. *The Journal of Applied Psychology, 102*(3) 530–545.

James-Ward, C. (2013). The coaching experience of four novice principals. *International Journal of Mentoring and Coaching in Education, 2*(1), 21–33.

Lee, L. (2015). School performance trajectories and the challenges for principal succession. *Journal of Educational Administration, 53*(2), 262–286.

Leithwood, K., Harris, A., & Hopkins, D. (2020). Seven strong claims about successful school leadership revisited. *School Leadership and Management, 40*(1), 5–22.

Levin, S., Bradley, K., & Scott, C. (2019). *Principal turnover: Insights from current principals.* Learning Policy Institute, National Association of Secondary School Principals. https://learningpolicyinstitute.org/product/nassp-principal-turnover-insights-brief

Levin, S., Scott, C., Yang, M., Leung, M., & Bradley, K. (2020). *Supporting a strong, stable principal workforce: What matters and what can be done.* Learning Policy Institute, National Association of Secondary School Principals. https://learningpolicyinstitute.org/product/supporting-strong-stable-principal-workforce-report

Lewis, P., & Murphy, R. (2008). New directions in school leadership. *School Leadership & Management, 28*(2), 127–146.

Liu, Y., & Bellibas, M. (2018). School factors that are related to school principals' job satisfaction and organizational commitment. *International Journal of Educational Research, 90*, 1–19.

Mahfouz, J. (2020). Principals and stress: Few coping strategies for abundant stressors. *Educational Management Administration & Leadership, 48*(3), 440–458.

Northfield, S. (2014). Multi-dimensional trust: How beginning principals build trust with their staff during leader succession. *International Journal of Leadership in Education, 17*(4), 410–441.

Parylo, O., & Zepeda, S. (2015). Connecting principal succession and professional learning: A cross-case analysis. *Journal of School Leadership, 25*(5), 940–968.

Postma, K., & Babo, G. (2019). The influence of self-efficacy on principal job satisfaction: A study of one northeastern USA state. *International Studies in Educational Administration, 47*(1), 74–88.

Shah, I. A., Fakhr, Z., Ahmad, M. S., & Zaman, K. (2010). Measuring push, pull and personal factors affecting turnover intention: A case of university teachers in Pakistan. *Review of Economic and Business Studies, 3*(1), 167–192.

Simkins, S., Close, P., & Smith, R. (2009) Work-shadowing as a process for facilitating leadership succession in primary schools. *School Leadership and Management, 29*(3), 239–251.

Snodgrass Rangel, V. (2018). A review of the literature on principal turnover. *Review of Educational Research, 88*(1), 87–124.

Stone-Johnson, C., & Weiner, J. (2020). Principal professionalism in the time of COVID-19. *Journal of Professional Capital and Community, 5*(34), 367–374.

Tekleselassie, A., & Choi, J. (2021). Understanding school principal attrition and mobility through hierarchical generalized linear modeling. *Educational Policy, 35*(7), 1116–1162.

Tekleselassie, A., & Villarreal, P. (2011). Career mobility and departure intentions among school principals in the United States: Incentives and disincentives. *Leadership and Policy in Schools, 10*, 251–293.

Tintore, M., Cunha, R., Cabral, I., & Alves, J. (2020). A scoping review of problems and challenges faced by school leaders (2003–2019). *Educational Management Administration & Leadership.* Epub ahead of print, August 12, 2020. http://doi.org/10.1177/1741143220942527

Tran, H., & Buckman D. (2017). The impact of principal movement and school achievement on principal salaries. *Leadership and Policy in Schools, 16*(1), 106–129.

Tran, H., McCormick, J., & Nguyen, T. (2018). The cost of replacing South Carolina high school principals. *Management in Education, 32*(3), 109–118.

Wang, F., Pollack, K., & Hauseman, C. (2018). School principals' job satisfaction: The effects of work intensification. *Canadian Journal of Educational Administration and Policy, 185*, 73–90.

Wilkerson, R. D., & Wilson, C. M. (2017). "Beating against the wind": The politics of race and retention in supporting African American principal advocacy and growth. *Journal of School Leadership, 27*(6), 772–799.

Yan, R. (2020). The influence of working conditions on principal turnover in K–12 public schools. *Educational Administration Quarterly, 56*(1) 89–122.

Zepeda, S., Bengtson, E., & Parylo, O. (2012). Examining the planning and management of principal succession. *Journal of Educational Administration, 50*(2), 136–158.

Chapter 7

Who Wants to Be a Principal?
Recruiting Instructional Leaders

Haim Shaked, Hemdat College of Education, Sdot Negev, Israel

In recent years, evidence has accumulated proving the importance of the school principal in promoting high academic achievement for students. In 2008, Leithwood et al. claimed that "school leadership is second only to classroom teaching as an influence on pupil learning" (Leithwood et al., 2008, p. 7). In 2020, they noted: "We considered this claim controversial at the time but have been surprised by its wide acceptance and endorsement within the leadership field. Indeed, this is one of the most frequently quoted claims we have made in our respective careers" (Leithwood et al., 2020, p. 6).

Moreover, Leithwood et al. noted that "as compared with 2008, there is now a much larger corpus of high-quality quantitative evidence available that demonstrates the ... contributions of school leadership to pupil learning, as well as the catalytic effects of such leadership on other consequential features of the school and its community" (2020, p. 6). Therefore, we now know with certainty that school leadership's effectiveness is crucial to improving student learning and results.

Particularly, to be effective in raising student achievement, principals must enact instructional leadership. Instructional leadership may be concisely explained as a school leadership approach that prioritizes teaching and learning development and therefore requires school leaders' extensive and direct involvement in improving instruction and curriculum (Glanz, 2022; Glickman et al., 2017; Neumerski et al., 2018).

Instructional leadership has been proven to have the most decisive positive impact on student outcomes in various school contexts and levels. Even after controlling for other variables such as student demographics, the principal's instructional leadership consistently accounts for significant variance in students' academic outcomes (e.g., Day et al., 2016; Hallinger & Wang, 2015; Hou et al., 2019; Shatzer et al., 2014).

However, recruiting principals who serve as instructional leaders is challenging, because those who are competent to serve as instructional leaders often do not want to become school principals (Doyle & Locke, 2014; Grissom et al., 2019). Cieminski (2018, p. 22) noted: "In recent years, the principal's role has changed from an administrator to an instructional leader. . . . During that time, major trends in the workforce included turnover at an 'unsustainable level.'" Hayes and Irby (2020, p. 131) claimed that the "instructional leadership mindset" is not sufficiently developed among those aspiring to school leadership.

This chapter aims to expand our understanding of the challenges of hiring instructional leaders as principals. The chapter will first conceptualize instructional leadership. Next, it will establish the importance of instructional leadership for candidates aspiring to be principals. Then, it will answer the most critical question: Why is it challenging to recruit principals who demonstrate instructional leadership, and what can be done?

WHAT IS INSTRUCTIONAL LEADERSHIP?

Of all the theories and models that the research literature on school leadership has proposed to describe how principals influence school performance, instructional leadership has been the most frequently studied conceptual framework over the past several decades (Hallinger et al., 2020; Hallinger & Wang, 2015). Instructional leadership is an educational leadership approach in which principals are continually and actively involved in a wide range of activities to improve teaching and learning for all students (Hallinger et al., 2020).

According to the instructional leadership approach, principals are expected to promote best instructional practices so that students can achieve academic success (Murphy et al., 2016; Neumerski, 2012). Principals should prioritize instruction and curriculum, while everything else—including traditional administrative and other tasks—should be considered less critical (Glanz, 2005).

Over the years, researchers have attempted to capture the meaning of instructional leadership through several frameworks. The framework presented by Hallinger and Murphy (1985) is the most commonly used in the instructional leadership research literature (Hallinger & Wang, 2015). It consists of three dimensions and ten functions.

In the first dimension, *defining the school mission*, the instructional leader is expected to be responsible for ensuring a clear mission for the school, which can be obtained by focusing on the academic progress of all students and by sharing this mission with the school community. This dimension asks the principal to perform two main functions: (1) framing the school's instructional goals, and (2) communicating those goals to all the necessary parties.

The second dimension, *managing the instructional program*, refers to the principal's ultimate responsibility for regulating and controlling the school's academic curricula. This dimension comprises three primary functions: (1) coordinating the school's curriculum, (2) supervising and evaluating instruction, and (3) monitoring students' progress.

The third dimension, *developing a positive school learning climate*, refers to the instructional leader's responsibility for creating a culture of ongoing improvement and high expectations for both students and teachers. This dimension is broken down into five functions for the school principal: (1) protecting instructional time from threats, (2) providing incentives to motivate teachers (3) providing incentives to encourage students' learning, (4) promoting staff members' continual professional development, and (5) maintaining high visibility to promote quality interactions with teachers and students.

Similar to the framework proposed by Hallinger and Murphy (1985), the one outlined by Weber (1996) delineates five dimensions of instructional leadership: (1) defining the school's mission, (2) managing curriculum and instruction, (3) supervising teaching, (4) monitoring student progress, and (5) assessing the instructional climate.

Based on a systematic and broad literature review, Stronge et al. (2008) summarized five essential features of instructional leadership that principals have been found to apply to meet instructional goals.

These features are outlined below:

1. *Building and sustaining a school vision:* developing a school vision that sets clear learning goals and gaining community support for those goals
2. *Sharing leadership:* distributing leadership roles by strengthening the expertise of teacher leaders to enhance school performance
3. *Leading a learning community:* steering a collaborative community of professional learners that provides meaningful staff development
4. *Using data to make instructional decisions:* collecting and using facts and evidence in instructional decision-making
5. *Monitoring curriculum and instruction:* tracking and promoting the implementation of curricula and quality teaching methods by spending time in classrooms

Blase and Blase (2000) explored teachers' perspectives on principals' instructional leadership, focusing on the link between instructional leadership and teachers. Based on an open-ended questionnaire, they identified two themes and eleven strategies of instructional leadership that influence changes in teacher practice.

The first theme was *talking with teachers to promote reflection*. This theme included five strategies: (1) making suggestions, (2) giving feedback, (3) modeling, (4) using inquiry and soliciting advice and opinions, and (5) giving praise.

The second theme was *promoting professional growth*. This theme incorporated six strategies: (1) emphasizing the study of teaching and learning; (2) supporting collaboration efforts among educators; (3) developing coaching relationships among educators; (4) encouraging and supporting the redesign of programs; (5) applying the principles of adult learning, growth, and development to all phases of staff development; and (6) implementing action research to inform instructional decision-making.

By examining these major instructional leadership frameworks, the salient points at the core of instructional leadership emerge and can be synthesized. Thus, the four key elements of instructional leadership are outlined below:

1. *Instructional vision:* building and mobilizing support for a school vision based on goals for student learning and results
2. *Instructional program:* coordinating, supervising, guiding, and monitoring teaching and learning in the school
3. *Instructional climate:* creating a positive, achievement-oriented academic environment
4. *Developing teachers:* ensuring that faculty members continue to strengthen their practice throughout their career

Table 7.1 illustrates how the various elements of instructional leadership discussed in the research on frameworks fall under the proposed four key elements of instructional leadership.

WHY SHOULD ASPIRING PRINCIPALS BECOME INSTRUCTIONAL LEADERS?

When recruiting a new school principal, there are many relevant considerations. However, it is of utmost importance to ensure that the principal will have a positive influence on student learning and achievement (Doyle & Locke, 2014; Grissom et al., 2019). Therefore, instructional leadership is a crucial prerequisite for principal candidates.

Table 7.1. The Proposed Four Key Elements of Instructional Leadership Deriving from the Prevalent Frameworks of Instructional Leadership

Key element	Hallinger & Murphy, 1985	Weber, 1996	Stronge et al., 2008	Blase & Blase, 2000
Instructional vision	Defining the school mission — Framing school goals; Communicating school goals	Defining the school mission	Building and sustaining a school vision	
Instructional program	Managing the instructional program — Coordinating the curriculum; Supervising and evaluating instruction	Managing curriculum and instruction; Supervising teaching	Monitoring curriculum and instruction; Using data to make instructional decisions	Making suggestions; Giving feedback; Modeling; Using inquiry and soliciting advice and opinions
Instructional climate	Developing a positive school learning climate — Monitoring student progress; Protecting instructional time; Providing incentives for teachers; Providing incentives for learning; Maintaining high visibility	Monitoring student progress; Assessing the instructional climate		Giving praise
Developing teachers	Promoting professional development		Leading a learning community; Promoting professional growth	Talking with teachers to promote reflection; Emphasizing the study of teaching and learning; Supporting collaboration efforts; Developing coaching relationships; Encouraging the redesign of programs; Applying the principles of adult learning, growth, and development; Implementing action research

Instructional leadership is based on the close relationships identified between teachers' quality of instruction and students' academic results (Murphy et al., 2016). Teaching quality may be seen as "one of the most important school-based resources in determining students' future academic success and lifetime outcomes" (Burroughs et al., 2019, p. 7), or even as "*the* most important variable affecting student achievement, even more so than demographic factors" (Seebruck, 2015, p. 1, emphasis in original).

A consistent finding across studies reveals that one standard deviation increase in teacher quality translates into approximately a 0.1–0.2 standard deviation gain in student achievement in elementary schools and a 0.2–0.4 standard deviation gain in student achievement in middle schools (Canales & Maldonado, 2018).

In light of the close connection between teaching quality and student performance, the instructional leadership approach is based on the understanding that the principal is charged with ensuring quality teaching in the school. As an instructional leader, the principal improves teaching quality through coordinating, monitoring, supervising, controlling, and evaluating teaching, because "an examination of instruction must be at the heart of the question of how leadership contributes to student learning" (Seashore Louis et al., 2010a, p. 321).

The influence of principals as instructional leaders on student learning and academic results is mainly indirect, mediated by factors such as the instructional program and the school culture, and most of all by the teachers' teaching strategies. Principals who enact instructional leadership make sure that teachers take full advantage of instructional time for effective, high-quality teaching and that teachers develop professionally on an ongoing basis (Goldring et al., 2015; Neumerski et al., 2018).

Research has affirmed the efficacy of instructional leadership with respect to reaching the goals of student achievement and school improvement (Day et al., 2016; Mitchell et al., 2015). A wide body of research literature associated instructional leadership with positive school outcomes, including higher teaching quality and improved student achievements. Even after controlling for other variables, such as student demographics, principals' instructional leadership consistently accounts for significant variance in students' academic outcomes (Hallinger & Wang, 2015; Hou et al., 2019).

Research studies have pinpointed instructional leadership as a pivotal function of principals who achieve promising school improvement outcomes. This link has been demonstrated in various organizational contexts such as in elementary, middle, and high schools as well as across public, private, and public charter schools. This connection has also been demonstrated in diverse geospatial contexts such as urban and suburban schools (Shatzer et al., 2014).

The link between instructional leadership and higher student achievement led scholars to issue a broadly voiced call for contemporary principals to make instructional leadership their top priority. School principals are expected and even required, to assume a prominent role as instructional leaders who emphasize the teaching and learning aspects of school leadership and are involved in a wide array of curricular and instructional issues (Glanz, 2005; Glickman et al., 2017).

Particularly, instructional leadership is needed for social justice. Unfortunately, factors such as race, gender, religion, national origin, ability or disability, and sexual orientation still determine the degree of academic success an individual can achieve (Francis et al., 2017). Two students with similar natural talent do not always get the same opportunities and reach the same results (Papa, 2020).

Instructional leadership contributes to reducing social injustice because it strives to lead all students to high academic performance, regardless of diverse students' potentially marginalizing characteristics. Instructional leadership is an equity-driven approach that promotes high levels of excellence for all students (Rigby, 2014; Shaked, 2020).

Based on the literature, we can definitely state that when recruiting new school principals, it is imperative to ensure that they are instructional leaders who contribute to student learning and outcomes. One of the most extensive in-depth studies of school leadership reported that "we have not found a single case of a school improving its student achievement record in the absence of talented leadership" (Seashore Louis et al., 2010b, p. 9). Without instructional leadership, principals cannot produce high-performing schools.

WHY IS RECRUITING INSTRUCTIONAL LEADERS CHALLENGING? AND WHAT CAN BE DONE?

In recent years, there has been an uptick in principal turnover, making it paramount for K–12 districts to focus on recruiting principals (Ni et al., 2015; Palmer, 2018; Tran, 2017). Despite the undeniable importance of instructional leadership, recruiting principals who are instructional leaders is not easy (Cieminski, 2018; Hayes & Irby, 2020). The current section aims to offer an explanation for why it is particularly challenging to hire principals who demonstrate instructional leadership, suggesting that this challenge is rooted in the prerequisite ability of instructional leadership—instructional expertise.

Instructional expertise is one of the fundamental capabilities needed to engage in effective instructional leadership (Robinson, 2010). Spillane and Seashore Louis (2002) claim that

> Without an understanding of the knowledge necessary for teachers to teach well—content knowledge, general pedagogical knowledge, content specific pedagogical knowledge, curricular knowledge and knowledge of learners—school leaders will be unable to perform essential school improvement functions such as monitoring instruction and supporting teacher development. (p. 97)

Many of a principal's activities aimed at promoting improved teaching methods and student achievement, such as setting instructional goals; speaking with teachers about the quality of teaching; and monitoring what is being taught, when, and how are virtually impossible to achieve without an understanding of how to create and facilitate effective teaching and learning environments for all students (Quebec Fuentes & Jimerson, 2020).

Researchers reported that the greater their instructional expertise, the more principals could attend to additional aspects of instruction, moving beyond surface features of instruction to underlying pedagogy and assessment (Lochmiller & Acker-Hocevar, 2016; Steele et al., 2015). Therefore, it is widely agreed that instructional expertise is needed to enact instructional leadership (Goldring et al., 2019; Murphy et al., 2016).

Herein lies the crux of the problem: To be an effective instructional leader, one needs to be proficient in teaching and learning, but those who are proficient in teaching and learning derive great satisfaction from doing so and do not easily give it up. Instructional expertise, which is needed for instructional leadership, is found in those who love teaching. And those who love teaching do not always want to replace it with school leadership.

Teachers see becoming a principal as leaving the teaching profession. As explained by Murphy et al. (2016, p. 462): "When school leaders 'left teaching,' they immediately set themselves up as something different from teachers and an occupation different from teaching. They were no longer teachers. . . . They were not in the teaching business. . . . They were managers and administrators."

From a teacher's perspective, running a school requires dealing with many things other than instruction and curricula. Therefore, those who enjoy teaching are not in a hurry to become principals. Recruiting principals who demonstrate instructional leadership requires recruiting those who, too often, do not want to leave teaching.

To address this challenge, the meaning of becoming a principal should be changed. Traditionally, principals "were not held accountable for teaching, learning, and outcomes for students" (Goldring et al., 2015, p. 22). They were evaluated both formally and informally according to their ability to keep order among students and calm between teachers and administrators, and between the school and the larger community, and were primarily responsible for keeping students safe, overseeing schedules, and enforcing school policies. "Managerial tasks such as ordering supplies and creating bus schedules were common daily tasks" (Glanz et al., 2017, p. 132).

Contrary to this traditional view, instructional leadership claims that when principals do not engage in the main component of schooling (i.e., the what and how of teaching and learning), they do not fulfill their mission. Instructional leadership aims to divert principals' attention away from administrative duties, logistical tasks, and disciplinary responsibilities to the core of schooling, which is teaching and learning. Principals are expected to be extensively and directly involved in this essential part of school life and are not allowed to settle for dealing with secondary issues only.

CONCLUSION

Let us suppose that potential principals do not see becoming a principal as leaving teaching, but instead, as receiving an opportunity to significantly influence teaching. In that case, instructional leaders may more readily agree to enter the principalship. We must create a reality in which being appointed principal does not require abandoning teaching, but rather, allows the new principal to have a broad impact on teaching and learning in the school. Only in this way can we bring those who love teaching and learning closer to school leadership positions.

REFERENCES

Blase, J., & Blase, J. (2000). Effective instructional leadership: Teachers' perspectives on how principals promote teaching and learning in schools. *Journal of Educational Administration, 38*(2), 130–141.

Burroughs, N., Gardner, J., Lee, Y., Guo, S., Touitou, I., Jansen, K., & Schmidt, W. (2019). A review of the literature on teacher effectiveness and student outcomes. *Teaching for Excellence and Equity, 6,* 7–17.

Canales, A., & Maldonado, L. (2018). Teacher quality and student achievement in Chile: Linking teachers' contribution and observable characteristics. *International Journal of Educational Development, 60,* 33–50.

Cieminski, A. B. (2018). Practices that support leadership succession and principal retention. *Education Leadership Review, 19*(1), 21–41.

Day, C., Gu, Q., & Sammons, P. (2016). The impact of leadership on student outcomes: How successful school leaders use transformational and instructional strategies to make a difference. *Educational Administration Quarterly, 52*(2), 221–258.

Doyle, D., & Locke, G. (2014). *Lacking leaders: The challenges of principal recruitment, selection, and placement.* Thomas B. Fordham Institute. https://files.eric.ed.gov/fulltext/ED545231.pdf

Francis, B., Mills, M., & Lupton, R. (2017). Towards social justice in education: Contradictions and dilemmas. *Journal of Education Policy, 32*(4), 414–431.

Glanz, J. (2005). *What every principal should know about instructional leadership.* Corwin.

Glanz, J. (2022). Personal reflections on supervision as instructional leadership: From whence it came and to where shall it go? *Journal of Educational Supervision, 4*(3). https://doi.org/10.31045/jes.4.3.5

Glanz, J., Shaked, H., Rabinowitz, C., Shenhav, S., & Zaretsky, R. (2017). Instructional leadership practices among principals in Israeli and USA Jewish schools. *International Journal of Educational Reform, 26*(2), 132–153.

Glickman, C. D., Gordon, S. P., & Ross-Gordon, J. M. (2017). *Supervision and instructional leadership: A developmental approach* (10th ed.). Pearson.

Goldring, E., Grissom, J. A., Neumerski, C. M., Murphy, J., Blissett, R., & Porter, A. (2015). *Making time for instructional leadership.* The Wallace Foundation. https://www.wallacefoundation.org/knowledge-center/pages/making-time-for-instructional-leadership.aspx

Goldring, E., Grissom, J. A., Neumerski, C. M., Blissett, R., Murphy, J., & Porter, A. (2019). Increasing principals' time on instructional leadership: Exploring the SAM® process. *Journal of Educational Administration, 58*(1), 19–37.

Grissom, J. A., Bartanen, B., & Mitani, H. (2019). Principal sorting and the distribution of principal quality. *AERA Open, 5*(2), 1–21.

Hallinger, P., & Murphy, J. (1985). Assessing the instructional management behavior of principals. *The Elementary School Journal, 86*(2), 217–247.

Hallinger, P., & Wang, W. C. (2015). *Assessing instructional leadership with the Principal Instructional Management Rating Scale.* Springer.

Hallinger, P., Gümüş, S., & Bellibaş, M. Ş. (2020). "Are principals instructional leaders yet?": A science map of the knowledge base on instructional leadership, 1940–2018. *Scientometrics, 122*(3), 1629–1650.

Hayes, S. D., & Irby, B. J. (2020). Challenges in preparing aspiring principals for instructional leadership: Voices from the field. *International Journal of Leadership in Education, 23*(2), 131–151.

Hou, Y., Cui, Y., & Zhang, D. (2019). Impact of instructional leadership on high school student academic achievement in China. *Asia Pacific Education Review, 20*(4), 543–558.

Leithwood, K., Harris, A., & Hopkins, D. (2008). Seven strong claims about successful school leadership. *School Leadership and Management, 28*(1), 27–42.

Leithwood, K., Harris, A., & Hopkins, D. (2020). Seven strong claims about successful school leadership revisited. *School Leadership & Management, 40*(1), 5–22.

Lochmiller, C. R., & Acker-Hocevar, M. (2016). Making sense of principal leadership in content areas: The case of secondary math and science instruction. *Leadership and Policy in Schools, 15*(3), 273–296.

Mitchell, R. M., Kensler, L. A., & Tschannen-Moran, M. (2015). Examining the effects of instructional leadership on school academic press and student achievement. *Journal of School Leadership, 25*(2), 223–251.

Murphy, J., Neumerski, C. M., Goldring, E., Grissom, J., & Porter, A. (2016). Bottling fog? The quest for instructional management. *Cambridge Journal of Education*, *46*(4), 455–471.

Neumerski, C. M. (2012). Rethinking instructional leadership, a review: What do we know about principal, teacher, and coach instructional leadership, and where should we go from here? *Educational Administration Quarterly*, *49*(2), 310–347.

Neumerski, C. M., Grissom, J. A., Goldring, E., Rubin, M., Cannata, M., Schuermann, P., & Drake, T. A. (2018). Restructuring instructional leadership: How multiple-measure teacher evaluation systems are redefining the role of the school principal. *The Elementary School Journal*, *119*(2), 270–297.

Ni, Y., Sun, M., & Rorrer, A. (2015). Principal turnover: Upheaval and uncertainty in charter schools? *Educational Administration Quarterly*, *51*(3), 409–437.

Palmer, B. (2018). It's time to upgrade to principal selection 2.0. *NASSP Bulletin*, *102*(3), 204–213.

Papa, R. (Ed.). (2020). *Handbook on promoting social justice in education*. Springer.

Quebec Fuentes, S., & Jimerson, J. B. (2020). Role enactment and types of feedback: The influence of leadership content knowledge on instructional leadership efforts. *Journal of Educational Supervision*, *3*(2), 6–31.

Rigby, J. G. (2014). Three logics of instructional leadership. *Educational Administration Quarterly*, *50*(4), 610–644.

Robinson, V. M. J. (2010). From instructional leadership to leadership capabilities: Empirical findings and methodological challenges. *Leadership and Policy in Schools*, *9*(1), 1–26.

Seashore Louis, K., Dretzke, B., & Wahlstrom, K. (2010a). How does leadership affect student achievement? Results from a national US survey. *School Effectiveness and School Improvement*, *21*(3), 315–336.

Seashore Louis, K., Leithwood, K., Wahlstrom, K. L., & Anderson, S. E. (2010b). *Learning from leadership: Investigating the links to improved student learning.* The Wallace Foundation. https://www.wallacefoundation.org/knowledge-center/Documents/Investigating-the-Links-to-Improved-Student-Learning.pdf

Seebruck, R. (2015). Teacher quality and student achievement: A multilevel analysis of teacher credentialization and student test scores in California high schools. *McGill Sociological Review*, *5*, 1–18.

Shaked, H. (2020). Social justice leadership, instructional leadership, and the goals of schooling. *International Journal of Educational Management*, *34*(1), 81–95.

Shatzer, R. H., Caldarella, P., Hallam, P. R., & Brown, B. L. (2014). Comparing the effects of instructional and transformational leadership on student achievement: Implications for practice. *Educational Management Administration & Leadership*, *42*(4), 445–459.

Spillane, J. P., & Seashore Louis, K. (2002). School improvement process and practices: Professional learning for building instructional capacity. In J. Murphy (Ed.) *The educational leadership challenge: Redefining leadership for the 21st century* (pp. 83–104). University of Chicago.

Steele, M. D., Johnson, K. R., Otten, S., Herbel-Eisenmann, B. A., & Carver, C. L. (2015). Improving instructional leadership through the development of leadership content knowledge: The case of principal learning in algebra. *Journal of Research on Leadership Education, 10*(2), 127–150.

Stronge, J. H., Richard, H. B., & Catano, N. (2008). *Qualities of effective principals*. Association for Supervision and Curriculum Development.

Tran, H. (2017). The impact of pay satisfaction and school achievement on high school principals' turnover intentions. *Educational Management Administration & Leadership, 45*(4), 621–638.

Weber, J. (1996). Leading the instructional program. In S. C. Smith & P. K. Piele (Eds.), *School leadership: Handbook for excellence* (2nd ed., pp. 191–224). ERIC Clearinghouse on Educational Management.

Chapter 8

Challenges Facing Principals
Voices From the Field

David Scanga and Renee Sedlack, Saint Leo University

Effective school leadership, and specifically principal leadership, is vital to the success of every school. The connection between school leadership and student achievement has been studied for decades. Students in the United States who have historically been marginalized or resided in low-income communities particularly benefit from dynamic school leadership (Illinois Principals Association, 2022). Schools require visionary leaders who create collaborative student-centered cultures, build leadership capacity among the staff, and focus on equity and inclusion for all students.

In a recent Wallace Foundation study, researchers concluded:

Across six rigorous studies estimating principals' effects using panel data, principals' contributions to student achievement were nearly as large as the average effects of teachers identified in similar studies. Principals' effects, however, are larger in scope because they averaged over all students in a school, rather than a classroom. (Grissom et al., 2021)

In addition, these researchers highlighted other studies that show that principals affect student absenteeism, teacher retention, and the ability to foster a positive learning and teaching environment. Principal turnover tends to negatively affect these dynamics and is particularly impactful in communities serving low-income students and students of color (Grissom et al., 2021).

The value of an effective principal can be measured by a productive school climate, the facilitation of a collaborative approach to instruction, and the strategic management of resources and personnel. Equity-focused principals enable schools to close achievement gaps and offer more positive outcomes for all students (Grissom et al., 2021). The importance of the role of the principal creates great concern today as the number of school leaders leaving the profession is increasing alarmingly.

The United States is experiencing a crisis in public school leadership, as one in two principals is considering retiring or a career change, according to a recent survey by the National Association of Secondary School Principals (Ward, 2022). The issues of work-life balance, salary, and lack of societal respect, among others, are cited as some of the main concerns facing principals today.

Throughout the nation, principals are frustrated by mounting accountability pressures, which take time away from supporting teachers and students, building capacity, and improving instructional practices. Multiple-measured teacher evaluation systems and the focus on student assessment as sole measures of quality have resulted in school leaders spending time on activities that do not contribute to positive student outcomes (Grissom et al., 2021).

Perhaps the most critical external pressure facing US principals is the political unrest in the nation. Political issues such as race relations, the rights of LGBTQ+ students, social and emotional learning, and students' access to books in the school library have resulted in conflicts between principals, parents, and community members (Turner, 2022). High levels of tension in communities have even created conflicts between students during the school day.

Recent major disruptions to school systems in every state are driven by the lingering effects of the COVID-19 pandemic as well as the changing economic, political, and social landscape. Principals are struggling to staff schools to offset educators leaving the profession. At the same time, new positions are being added to help students recoup learning losses due to the pandemic and to stem an increasing mental health crisis (Camera, 2022). Across the United States, school districts continue to have unfilled vacancies, so principals often find themselves in teaching roles.

These factors contribute to the lack of educators who view the principalship as a viable career path. Principal attrition combined with a dwindling principal pipeline is causing school systems to examine practices for principal support and retention (Illinois Principals Association, 2022). Examining this issue and listening to voices in the field for guidance to craft solutions is worthwhile and is the purpose of this chapter.

LISTENING TO VOICES OF PRINCIPALS FROM THE FIELD

As described above, the internal and external pressures on school organizations, particularly on principals, combine to create a highly charged educational climate. Some change initiatives can be traced to current events, such as the political unrest in the nation; however, some change initiatives have a historical context that can be traced over decades. The "effective schools movement" of the 1970s and 1980s brought definitive research that showed fundamental changes were needed for school improvement and success.

Efforts to improve effectiveness in schools and classrooms have been a focus of educational institutions, especially in schools serving diverse student populations. According to effective school research, an effective school has an instructional leader, not a manager; a strong culture driven by a vision; high-quality instruction; high expectations for all students; strong accountability measures; and a safe learning environment (Cuban, 2018; Salazar, 2020).

The pressure brought on by the effective schools movement forced an internal change in structures and roles. Effective school research highlighted the role of the principal in developing comprehensive systems that resulted in positive outcomes for all students. Principals became directly responsible for all students achieving despite their backgrounds, learning challenges, or lack of parental support.

As a result, over the past several decades, the principal's role has become a high-stakes, emotionally taxing, overwhelming position with immense responsibility. The unintended consequence of role changes was principal turnover and mobility, which undercut what the effective school movement hoped to achieve. The school principal, as research has found, is second only to teachers when it comes to their direct impact on student learning and achievement outcomes (Bryk & Schneider, 2003). Creating stability in the ranks of principals is necessary if positive school change is to be achieved.

As long-time practitioners in the field of education, both authors have served as principals; we know the importance of paying attention to the challenges school principals face. A principal's longevity in the position allows for positive change to take place in a school over years of service. Disruption in a principal's journey ripples through a school and its district, creating negative fallout that must be addressed by the next in line. School districts should pay attention to the challenges and worries that both novice and existing principals report to increase the probability that newly appointed principals will succeed.

The following is a combination of research in the literature and three studies involving principals' perspectives on their lived experiences in a mid-size district in central Florida. All three studies gathered perceptions of what principals are saying about the challenges of the job and what they need to be successful. Listening to principals in the field, many of whom have only one to three years of experience, will highlight significant barriers and challenges to be overcome. Exploring ways to sustain leadership is an excellent place to start if we hope to achieve sustainable school improvement.

Considering the challenges of accepting the principal role, why does anyone agree to lead a school? The truth is that despite the responsibility and stress of the position, principals who enter the fray continue to express compassion and motivation to make a difference in the lives of students, teachers, and parents. A principal refrain often heard is, "I chose to be a principal, so I could lead a school and make a direct impact on students' lives."

Out of a group of 40 elementary school principals asked to respond to the statement "I like the job I have as principal," 82% agreed or strongly agreed with the statement. This is despite 55% of the same group reporting high stress levels (Berryhill, 2021). Successful principals have a strong sense of purpose and commitment to those they serve. A leader is undeniably attracted to the potential to positively impact students, teachers, staff, and the school community.

Literature is abundant on the subject of what principals need to succeed (Fullan, 2014). While this literature paints a general picture of how the principalship has changed and why individuals succeed or fail, research on school leadership is a moving target. Listening to current principals in the field generates new perspectives on common and uncommon issues that principals face daily in school settings. This is why listening to current principals is so essential.

Listening to principals illuminates where principals spend their time and energy and what creates anxiety and stress for them. We know that stress is a disabler and part of the reason principals say they leave the field or struggle to meet their full potential. Knowing their thoughts, beliefs, and assumptions will help school districts to build supports that help address principals' common issues and provide for their well-being.

Principals repeatedly express the commonality of the experience of leading a school. At a recent meeting of principals, one person reflected on this shared experience: "I thought I was alone in some of my thoughts this year, and it was nice to hear others having the same feelings." Building suitable support systems starts with listening to principals in the field. We learn that when principals come together, they recognize they are "all in the same boat" and "are learning together as they go." What are principals, new and old, saying about their current challenges?

Steinacker (2022) found in her work with new principals that challenges included understanding their new school's established culture and routines, creating a partnership with their assistant principal, navigating a plethora of new information, and learning how to let go of what they found familiar. Themes for all principals include comments about poor working conditions, lack of professional development opportunities, lack of autonomy, and the pressures of high-stakes testing (Levin & Bradley, 2019; Steinacker, 2022).

SPECIFIC CHALLENGES FOR PRINCIPALS

A common belief is that it takes a principal three years to implement systems and feel some level of ownership as a leader in a new school. During this time, a principal will face various challenges related to culture, personnel, finance, and student achievement, to name only a few of the likely difficulties.

Beyond three years, a principal continues to build on early initiatives and relationships; however, the work is never completed. Each year brings different challenges and renewed efforts to create effective systems that sustain efforts for school improvement. While schools are unique, we find through conversations with school leaders that common themes emerge that almost all principals face. Five themes regarding what is most challenging for principals surfaced from an analysis of the three studies that are the focus of this chapter. Principal statements supporting each theme are taken directly from the recent studies conducted in a central Florida school district.

Theme #1: What do principals say they like about instructional leadership?

- *Watching students succeed and helping families and colleagues to create success for students brings a sense of accomplishment.*
- *Seeing growth in students [who] no one else believes in*
- *The love from the children and knowing I am working as their advocate and voice to better their lives and our community*
- *Working with kids and helping them overcome the obstacles in their lives so they can believe there's hope for their future*
- *The ability to determine the teaching teams for our school, how PD is led, [and] determine [the] needs of each teacher and work to coach them up*

However, there is a proverbial two-edged sword: Principals say they love the opportunity to lead as instructional leaders, but at the same time, instructional leadership takes an enormous amount of time and energy. The responsibility of instructional leadership weighs heavily on all leaders.

Like the famous line in the 1986 movie *Top Gun*, "I feel a need for speed," a principal would passionately say, "I feel a need to succeed" as an instructional leader. Principals agree that success in student achievement is the number one priority and one of the greatest stress producers. Results on accountability measures can dramatically change how a principal is perceived, putting enormous pressure on quality instructional leadership.

The instructional leadership role encompasses the principal's work to establish the vision and mission of the organization, high-quality instruction and curricula, and the promotion of a positive learning environment that includes feedback loops to monitor success (Fullan, 2014). Over the years, principals have accepted this responsibility knowing that they play a crucial role in developing a culture that responds to the needs of all children and the community of stakeholders associated with the school.

Principals expressed high levels of job satisfaction in the instructional leadership role. They are attracted to the opportunity to influence students, teachers, staff, and the community. Among the challenges of instructional leadership are analyzing classroom practices, building intervention systems, aligning curricula with standards, and changes in instructional practices (Salazar, 2020). Despite the enormous expectations placed on the school instructional leaders, principals accept the responsibility. One principal noted, "I love helping teachers grow professionally and students grow academically," and another noted that "I like holding my school family to high expectations and working for *all* students."

Theme #2: What are principals saying about autonomy?

- *Being able to be autonomous in the decision-making process [within] my school, I am able to better meet the needs of our school community, as each school's needs are different.*
- *I feel that I have [the freedom] to make the best decisions based on my students' and staffs' needs.*
- *[It's important to have] autonomy to make decisions for the betterment of the school.*
- *The thing I appreciate most is the amount of autonomy in my current position. We are allowed to do our best work for our kids each day.*
- *Principals should be allowed to make instructional decisions based on the needs of their schools.*
- *School demographics throughout the district are different; the "one size fits all" method is not working for all schools.*

Principals in these studies share the need for more autonomy as leaders. Autonomy gives principals the power to decide based on the school's local context. Principals clearly understand that much of their work is directed by outside sources, including the district and levels of government (local, state, and federal). However, having the autonomy to adapt how initiatives are implemented is highly engaging and increases the probability of teacher and staff acceptance. Having control over how things are done is a motivator for principals.

While autonomy showed up in all three studies, Berryhill (2021) specifically asked principals about their perception of their autonomy as school leaders.

Survey questions asked about various adaptive and technical issues and whether principals felt a degree of autonomy in making decisions. Principals generally felt a degree of autonomy when working in the areas of teacher development and student discipline, but feel the presence of the district when it comes to policies and procedures that need to be followed. What is important here is whether the principal can adjust when circumstances call for a different approach, such as in the areas of teacher development or student discipline.

This is where principals need help knowing when to adapt or push back on strict adherence to district procedures based on local contexts. Principals wish to be trusted to make decisions based on school-level conditions. While many principals (60%) say they feel trusted, others hope for increased autonomy and trust as they make school decisions (Berryhill, 2021).

Theme #3: What are principals saying about feeling isolated and overwhelmed by their responsibilities?

- *I thought I was alone, and it was nice to hear others [have] the same feelings.*
- *I wish I would have known how lonely this felt because then I could have tackled that ahead of time . . . people told me [and] I just did not listen.*
- *A year and a half later, maybe it is because you do not realize what to expect . . . you think you know, and then you get in the role, and you are like, "oh, I did not think about that part."*
- *[It's important to understand] the power of your time . . . people always want the principal.*
- *[It's difficult to know] how to provide when you are drowning . . . I can barely find my own dang checklist to keep track of, let alone try to make [one] for someone else.*

Principals understand the high demands of work and responsibility that come with the position. What they often need to anticipate is the corresponding need for personal well-being. Spillane & Lee (2014) discuss the "reality shock" implications of having ultimate responsibility for everything and everyone. The themes of isolation, loneliness, and responsibility are constant in the conversations with principals. They are, after all, at the top of the pyramid and the only ones with the title of principal. All decisions ultimately end up on the principal's desk, and they are held responsible for the outcomes of their decisions (Spillane & Lee, 2014).

It is little wonder that stress levels are high when principals feel alone and overwhelmed. Principals say they are always "turned on" at work and home seven days a week. The constant barrage of communication, whether in person or through social media platforms, makes it difficult to disconnect. Spillane and Lee (2014) make it clear in this statement: "Principal work also tends to be fragmented, fast-paced, and varied; it involves long hours and a relentless workload, along with demands from multiple, diverse stakeholders" (p. 432).

An interesting caveat related to the responsibility of principals is a recent shift in the field of education to reconsider the "why" or purpose of school (Snyder, 2015). While accountability measures like high-stakes testing still reign, there is a movement to instead prioritize students' preparation for their careers and future. One principal comment, "Leadership is so much more than accountability for performance and test scores—it really comes back to our purpose, why do we exist?" suggests that the idea of why we do what we do is now a topic of educational conversation.

Theme #4: What are principals saying about capacity building?

- *In a principal work group, I learned about the things I sometimes do naturally, but it was nice to see that there were other ways to approach situations that I haven't seen expressed so clearly [before].*
- *I love supporting teachers and building a collaborative culture.*
- *Working with teachers—instructional leadership, problem-solving, supporting professional development. Knowing the structures of the school to know where to begin. I think it is a struggle for all of us.*
- *We want to fix yesterday.*
- *Implementation of district initiatives [was previously] done differently, making it challenging to move the culture of the school forward. I did not know where to begin.*

There are no shortcuts when it comes to areas of expertise that principals must have to accomplish their role. Having expertise and knowledge in various structures and processes or knowing where to go for information is challenging for every principal. And while initially principals want to "fix" everything, they learn that a team approach is the only way to succeed.

The challenge for the principal is building systems that allow work to be completed and decisions to be made that are aligned with the vision but not dependent on one person, namely the principal. An effective school ultimately operates through a team approach using leaders across the school. However, to build collaborative systems, the principal must first build capacity in team members, ensuring vision alignment and knowledge of the policies and procedures needed to complete tasks.

Principals will tell you that building systems and the capacity to accomplish work as a team is a full-time job. Upon reflection, principals often say they must start with themselves, first learning how to cultivate leadership in others and second learning how to delegate power so they are not solely responsible for all decisions.

Theme #5: What are principals saying about trusting and relationships?

- *I love the impact we can have and the relationships we build with students, staff, and families.*
- *The culture in my building was positive and provided hope for our future.*
- *Students, community, and staff relationships—I am a person who values and prioritizes the human element of the purpose of our work.*
- *Overall, we need to be trusted and accountable as principals, but there must be some flexibility for us to do our jobs better.*

Principals understand from day one that relationships must be developed with teachers, staff, parents, and students. As a professional organization, a school depends on relational trust among all stakeholders for its success (Bryk & Schneider, 2003). Relational trust creates a shared purpose that animates education professionals to engage in collaborative work focused on community goals.

A principal new to a school begins the journey tabula rasa—with a clean slate. After the first day, everything said and done by the principal either builds trust or creates barriers to trusting relationships. Principals talk about the context of the school they inherited. The staff and faculty loved the previous principal (maybe for the wrong reasons), or they were happy to see the last administrator leave, hoping the next one would improve the situation. Principals feel pressure to make the right decisions early on and hope to build connections that will mutually serve all parties.

Building relational trust is the foundation for everything a principal does; however, this is an area of tremendous growth for most leaders. It is easy to get consumed with the technical and managerial parts of the job and not pay attention to the relational aspects of the job (Abbamont, 2020; Tschannen-Moran & Gareis, 2004). Day-to-day leadership exchanges result in trust built over time and the likelihood that people will work together to create a positive work culture.

CONCLUSION

When principals reflect on the enormity of the job that faces them every day, it is evident that they are certainly up to the challenge, if district support aligns with the needs they identify as critical for them to be successful. District support and respect are essential to help principals navigate the complexity of their role.

As we discussed early in the chapter, internal and external pressures distract the principal from focusing on instructional leadership. Accountability requirements from state and federal mandates force principals to spend countless hours on tasks unrelated to the main job functions that initially attracted them to the job.

A key component of principal retention is the notion of autonomy to determine what is best for the community served and to meet the needs of students. Building capacity among staff to provide insight into these decisions through trusting relationships will enable principals to create a sustainable network of support within the school and a common focus. Expanding this network of support to colleagues across the school district will provide a natural avenue for processing stressful situations and seeking possible solutions that were successful in other schools to build principals' capacity to lead.

The school leadership crisis in the United States is alarming. There is a critical need to support the dedicated principals we have in our schools. Listening to voices from the field is a powerful way to facilitate changes and to recruit and retain leaders who are critical to the education of our nation's children.

REFERENCES

Abbamont, G. W. (2020). *The new principal's journey: The experiences, challenges, and supports that contribute to the development of effective novice principals.* (Publication No. 27744319) [Doctoral dissertation, University of Pennsylvania]. ProQuest Dissertations & Theses Global.

Berryhill, T. (2021). *Factors impacting elementary retention: Job satisfaction, school context, and autonomous decision-making.* (Publication No. 13425867) [Doctoral dissertation, Saint Leo University]. ProQuest Dissertations & Theses Global.

Bryk, A. S., & Schneider, B. (2003). Trust in schools: A core resource for school reform. *Creating Caring Schools, 60*(6), 40–45.

Camera, L. (2022). *Half of principals eyeing career change.* US News and World Report. https://www.usnews.com/news/education-news/articles/2022-08-17/half-of-principals-eyeing-career-change-survey

Cuban, L. (2018). *Whatever happened to effective schools?* https://larrycuban.wordpress.com/2018/06/03/whatever-happened-to-effective-schools/

Fullan, M. (2014). *The principal: Three keys to maximizing impact*. John Wiley & Sons.

Grissom, J., Egalite, A., & Lindsay, C. (2021). *How principals affect students and schools: A systemic synthesis of two decades of research*. The Wallace Foundation. http://www.wallacefoundation.org/principalsynthesis

Illinois Principals Association. (2022). *Effective and sustained principals for every Illinois community*. https://ilprincipals.org/wp-content/uploads/2022/01/Effective-and-Sustained-Principals-6-2022-update.pdf

Levin, S., & Bradley, K. (2019). *A review of the research: Understanding and addressing principal turnover*. Learning Policy Institute, National Association of Secondary School Principals. https://learningpolicyinstitute.org/media/326/download?inline&file=NASSP_LPI_Principal_Turnover_Research_Review_REPORT.pdf

Salazar, A. (2020). *A phenomenology: Novice principals' perception of early challenges, best practices, strategies, and support systems*. (Publication No. 28319172) [Doctoral dissertation, San Diego State University]. ProQuest Dissertations & Theses Global.

Snyder, K. (2015). Engaged leaders develop schools as quality organizations. *InternationalJournal of Quality and Service Sciences, 7*(2/3), 217–229.

Spillane, J. P., & Lee, L. C. (2014). Novice school principals' sense of ultimate responsibility: Problems of practice in transitioning to the principal's office. *Educational Administration Quarterly, 50(3),* 431–465.

Steinacker, C. (2022). *Supportive practices for novice principals*. [Unpublished doctoral dissertation, Saint Leo University]. ProQuest Dissertations & Theses Global.

Tschannen-Moran, M., & Gareis, C. (2004). Principals' sense of efficacy: Assessing a promising construct. *Journal of Educational Administration, 42,* 573–585.

Turner, C. (2022). *School principals say culture wars made last year "rough as hell."* National Public Radio. https://www.npr.org/2022/12/01/1139685828/schools-democracy-misinformation-purple-state

Ward, M. (2022). *Survey: 50% of principals are stressed out to the point of quitting*. District Administration. https://districtadministration.com/survey-50-percent-of-principals-are-stressed-out-to-the-point-of-quitting/

Chapter 9

Initiatives to Support Principals in the Early Years of their Careers

Shmuel Shenhav, Michlalah Jerusalem College

A fundamental premise of this chapter is that effective recruitment and retention of principals depends on the alignment of three stages: preparation (Darling-Hammond, 2012), mentoring (Gimbel & Kefor, 2018), and induction (Wilmore, 2004), leading to proficiency during the early years of the principalship. Each stage is critical and dependent on the other. First, candidates for the principalship need a preparation program that combines the theories of school leadership with the practical realities of life as a principal. Research indicates that an effective program is one that reflects the latest theories and practices in school leadership (Zepeda, 2008).

The perennial divide between theory and practice is eschewed in the best preparation programs. Effective programs are framed after Kurt Lewin's (Hussain et al., 2018) famous statement, and I paraphrase, that there is no sound theory without practice, and no good practice that is not framed by some theory.

Second, once they complete through a theory- and practice-based preparation program, principals need support as they acclimate to their new role. Such mentoring is not unlike teacher mentoring (Fullan, 2001), which provides ongoing communication, feedback, and commitment to the relationship. As new principals progress through their first few years, continued induction into their role is necessary. This component is often neglected (Beycioglu & Wildy, 2017).

Mentoring, usually offered during the first two or three years of service, involves one-on-one support, while induction, a more expansive process over years three to five, entails several other strategies to support principals—including, for instance, continued professional development and intervisitations, to be explained later.

The issue of the gaps between the content of the preparation programs for school principals and the knowledge principals actually need in the position requires a multidimensional critique as this has been a perennial problem (Hess & Kelly, 2007). Graduates of principal preparation programs often confirm the perception that they are not fully prepared to meet the realities of school leadership (Grissom et al., 2019).

The model described and advocated in this chapter remedies this mismatch. Integral to this model is the candidate's identity as a leader (Cruz-Gonzalez et al., 2021), including their leadership style (Murphy, 2019); their perception of the role; and the knowledge, skills, and abilities that characterize the person and position (Devos & Bouckenooghe, 2009). These are fundamental aspects of an effective preparation program (Lynch, 2012).

To advance beyond one's preparation for the principalship, additional knowledge, skills, and dispositions must be addressed in mentorship while one is on the job (Wasonga & Murphy, 2006). Extant wisdom of the field, including its knowledge base and skills, its approaches to problem-solving, and the concepts of leadership expected by educational authorities (e.g., ministries of education) form a basis for mentoring. During this phase, experiential learning is connected with the theories gained in preparation programs.

Candidates faced with the exigencies of leadership are pressed to find solutions to seemingly intractable problems that frame the life of a school principal (Alsbury & Hackmann, 2006; Gordon, 2022). These experiences and practices during mentoring are further bolstered through the induction process (Nasser-Abu Alhija & Fresko, 2014).

This chapter presents the case for an alignment among preparation, mentoring, and induction that goes a long way toward improving the recruitment and retention of school principals. Initially, the chapter focuses on the disconnect between common preparation programs and the actual needs of school principals, especially in the early years of their careers.

The literature review will present current thinking in the field on leadership and the processes for preparing school principals based on their knowledge base, goals, and skills developed, as well as by the content and experiences prescribed by the program. After that, the chapter presents a program in Israel that provides continued professional growth of principals through mentoring and induction (Capstones, 2016).

THE PROFESSIONAL PREPARATION OF SCHOOL PRINCIPALS

The literature on principal preparation is prodigious and reviewing it in all its facets is beyond the purposes of this chapter. As indicated above, preparation has been lacking, primarily in its disconnect to the world of practice. In other words, too many preparation programs of old did not sufficiently address the realities of practicing principals (Brown, 2006; New Leaders, 2012).

One of the consequences of this omission was the emergence of alterative principal preparation programs that, realizing the deficiency of many traditional programs, offered more practical on-site preparation (Pannell et al., 2015). Candidates had the opportunity to put into practice many of the theories they learned in traditional coursework in college. These alternative programs gained popularity in the latter part of the last century, and have continued somewhat into the new century (Acker-Hocevar & Cruz-Janzen, 2008).

More recently, preparation and professional development of school principals in general, and in Israel in particular, have focused on the importance of instructional leadership. This emphasis is in part attributed to the awareness that school leaders' primary work in schools should focus on improving teaching and learning, which match the realities of school leadership today (Shaked, 2021).

This preparation focuses on three areas:

1. improving the supervisory knowledge and skills of principals and their assistants based on cutting-edge technologies in instructional leadership that are intended to improve teaching practice;
2. developing a schoolwide professional development plan aimed at improving classroom-based instruction by focusing on teaching practices and curricular processes so that all students achieve appropriate levels of performance; and
3. incorporating other instructional leadership initiatives such as action research, peer coaching, critical friends, and meaningful walk-throughs, all of which deepen the school's commitment to a culture of instructional excellence (Glickman et al., 2017).

According to Shaked (2021), instructional leadership is an educational leadership model in which principals are directly and continually involved in curricular and instructional issues. His study attempts to provide a basis for instructional leadership work in four areas: (1) with leaders themselves, (2) with mid-level school leaders, (3) with teachers, and (4) with external stakeholders.

Shaked's work is representative of current research and literature in the field. Current thinking conceives instructional leadership as part of the larger theoretical framework known as educational leadership. In other words, educational leadership, as demonstrated by a review of the literature in extant books and journals, encompasses many broader areas including, among others, leaders who work in varied contexts, not just schools, and leaders who lead in multifaceted ways including managing the organization, engaging in fundraising initiatives, and addressing financial and legal matters. Instructional leadership, in contrast, directly relates to practical matters related to the instructional process and is viewed as one particular arena in which educational leaders may operate (Glanz, 2022).

In Israel there has been a greater realization of the import of instructional leadership (Capstones, 2016). The principal serves as the head of the school's instructional hierarchy, and is concerned not only with leading the students to high-quality achievements and learning outcomes (Male & Palaiologou, 2012), but also with the professional growth of teachers so that they improve their teaching and lead learning processes in the classroom (Forssten-Seiser, 2020). Buzo-Schwartz and Mandel-Levi (2016) describe instructional leadership as the school principal's responsibility for leading and improving the teaching and learning processes:

> The processes for improving teaching through leading teachers' professional learning are complex, and they require expertise. The leadership practice that has the most impact on improving student achievement is the creation of formal and informal opportunities for learning processes and the professional development of teachers with the participation of the principal as a learner and as a leader. (p. 4)

Emphasis on the principal's role as an instructional leader, which is to strengthen and deepen the instructional skills and knowledge of the staff and to create a school culture of sharing knowledge and using it cooperatively, lends itself nicely to addressing the dichotomy between theory and practice.

The emphasis of instructional leadership in preparation programs matches the ever-increasing expectations of principals to deal directly with the teaching-learning process in schools. In this way, there's a greater match between real-world necessities (i.e., for instructional leadership) and traditional graduate courses in leadership (Shaked, 2022).

Another focal point in the professional development of principals is the desire for practical experience in leading change as an essential and central skill required of the school principal (Shahaf et al., 2011). In the conception of the preparation processes of school administrators, the field experience of principal candidates should be directed toward leading change in the school

(Capstones, 2021). The issue of leading change, apart from being related to the very core of principal work, deals with practical ways of bridging the gap between theories of change with the realities on the ground (Hurst, 2021).

Action research finds great relevance in this context. Action research, a special form of research that is now widely practiced by school personnel (i.e., teachers and other school leaders), provides principal candidates with the tools necessary to better understand the daily challenges they will face in schools. Action research affords principals the opportunity to reflect on their work experiences and obtain results (Schon, 1992/2017). For principal candidates, this action research practice is less about getting results than it is about understanding the process of creating change, an empowering and invaluable experience that allows principal candidates to reflect on practice.

There has been an emphasis on improving principal preparation by matching preparation with practical school-related activities and processes. The general research literature also points to the need for and value of bridging the gap between theory and practice once a candidate is assigned or appointed as principal through a mentoring program.

In a study conducted in the United States of mentors of novice principals, Bertrand et al. (2018) found four elements that create an effective mentorship and professional growth process: relevance (professional development that matches the reality in the school), shared goals, mutual trust, and a period of about two years of mentoring upon entering the position. Induction is a process that continues beyond the mentoring phase and further supports the principal to achieve greater levels of proficiency on the job (Brooks & Heffernan, 2020).

There are additional foci that must be considered in the professional development of school principals, such as developing personal and interpersonal skills, forging a professional identity and value-driven ideology, learning to make ethical decisions, and building an organizational infrastructure. These are worthy of discussion in future studies.

THE CURRENT REALITY OF SCHOOL PRINCIPAL PREPARATION IN ISRAEL

To highlight the importance of connecting preparation, mentorship, and induction, this section focuses on Israeli school principals. Although the context is unique, parallels to principals in other countries can be drawn. The national school system in Israel serves about 1.6 million students, with approximately 73% in the Jewish sector and 27% in the Arab sector (Israeli Central Bureau of Statistics, 2013).

Capstones (2008), which is the Israeli school leadership institute that spearheads school principal development in Israel, has defined the primary role of Israeli school principals as that of serving as instructional leaders in order to improve all students' education and learning. Four additional areas of management support this function: designing the school's future image by developing a vision and bringing about change; leading the staff and nurturing its professional development; focusing on the individual; and managing the relationship between the school and its surrounding community (Capstones, 2008).

Currently, Capstones (2021), in collaboration with the Israeli Ministry of Education (like boards of education in the United States), regulates and oversees all professional development programs for principal candidates and active principals. The program highlights desired principles, content areas, and skill sets in principal preparation.

The program emphasizes four core principles:

1. the importance of instructional leadership as a means to enhance school improvement
2. the need to bridge theory and practice through experiential learning
3. the development of a personal professional identity
4. orientation to the principalship

The program emphasizes seven content areas:

1. the development of an educational and ethical value-driven ideology
2. the importance of leading the professional development of teachers
3. the importance of leading the relationship between the school and the community
4. leadership based on data
5. the assessment of needs and building a work program to meet those needs
6. the need to design a schoolwide educational vision with a focus on the future
7. aspects of building and leading an organizational infrastructure

The program emphasizes five skill sets:

1. leading the learning processes in the school
2. leading the improvement of the instructional program in the school
3. gaining interpersonal skills
4. gaining personal skills
5. gaining knowledge and incorporating an ideology

These principles, content areas, and skill sets in the principal preparation program in Israel (as per Capstones, 2021) point to an optimal professional growth process aimed at developing a professionally mature principal who is capable of leadership that respects the classical aspects of the principalship yet is open to change and innovative practices.

Principles and trends in such areas as instructional leadership and leadership identity are reflected in the core content of professional development. Much emphasis is placed on establishing an educational ideology, learning data-based management, learning how to make decisions based on essential educational truisms, and building a professional vision. These principles and content areas are reinforced by those skill sets most needed for successful school administration.

This structure of principal preparation is meant to bridge the gap between theory and practice from the initial stage of preparation to on-the-job mentoring and induction during the first five years of serving as a principal (Villiani, 2014). This aligned and structured approach to support principals is aimed at recruiting and retaining effective principals. A strategic vision and organized plan aid in both recruitment and retention.

More practically and specifically, the process involved in recruiting Israeli school principals starts with a candidate possessing a bachelor's and master's degree approved by the Ministry of Education, preferably in educational administration. One cannot, however, assume a principalship without further professional principal preparation.

Capstones (2009), the Israeli school leadership institute that oversees this recruitment and professional development process, requires, as of this writing, that principal candidates undertake a special principal preparation course (referred to here as the Preparation Course for Principals, or in Hebrew *Course Menhalim*), which is fundamentally based on the principles, content areas, and skill sets enumerated above. After successfully completing this course, candidates are eligible to apply for principal vacancies and undergo a traditional interview process.

Aside from the fact that many candidates, for a variety of reasons beyond the scope of this chapter, do not end up applying for the many principal vacancies that exist, the problem is exacerbated by the theory-practice gap referred to earlier in the chapter. The principal course sponsored by Capstones is not as successful as it could be because it is conducted separately from the school setting in which future principals will work.

In other words, preparing principals outside the school setting provides for an artificial and unrealistic experience. As a result, several changes have been advocated and are described in the next section of this chapter.

A SHIFT IN THE RECRUITMENT AND PREPARATION OF PRINCIPALS

Principal preparation, whether it occurs in a traditional master's degree in educational administration at a local college or university, or in a special post-degree preparation course as described above (the Capstones model in Israel), is destined to be lacking or deficient because it is divorced from the realities that a principal faces in an actual school setting. Moreover, the Capstones (2009) curriculum itself has several dichotomies and inconsistencies that further diminish the effective preparation of future principals.

For instance, the Capstones program's principles, content areas, and skill sets explained above are not necessarily consistently aligned. We find some topics that are included in the program's content but are not found at the end of the process when assessing the skills of principals who completed the preparation program.

In addition, the important principle that a potential leader must examine their leadership identity or style is not fully discussed or represented in learning activities later in the preparation program. From the other end of the spectrum, the ethics and values highlighted in the content areas are not reflected in the list of guiding principles, nor do they appear in the skill set part of the program.

These discrepancies, among others, reflect one of the major weaknesses of the Israeli program of principal preparation. Other scholars and practitioners have similarly documented inconsistencies in the planning curriculum for principals at the preparation stage (Roegman & Woulfin, 2019). Most fundamental is the disconnect between the curricula taught in such programs and in graduate programs at universities and the day-to-day realities that a principal candidate will face on the job.

Therefore, as has been done elsewhere (Slater & Nelson, 2013), a closer tie between theories of school administration and practical leadership experience is being made in terms of the elimination of the preparation course prior to appointment as a principal. Under the new plan, a candidate would be eligible to assume the principalship without any preparation beyond their basic education degrees. Rather, after an interview process, a principal candidate would be placed in a principalship and only then receive the preparation course along with other newly appointed principals. They would also receive one-on-one mentoring in their own school.

The idea is that the principles, content areas, and skills sets they are exposed to in the preparation course should almost immediately be translated or transferred to the practical challenges and other realities they face in their very own school.

This new model was first articulated and supported by Luboshitz (2018), who proposed that the standard principal search and placement process and the preliminary preparation programs be cancelled. Instead, he suggested appointing principals through a local interview process that included officials from the Ministry of Education and then providing principal candidates the support necessary to be successful on the job.

This new model has several advantages over the former approach to recruiting principals. First, it was found that many individuals in the preparation program, for a variety of reasons, decided not to become principals. Thus, the time and cost involved in principal preparation were not only prohibitive for candidates, but also inefficient in recruiting candidates. Officials of Capstones felt that a more focused approach of preparing candidates who truly aspire to the principalship would be financially and practically more efficient and effective.

Also, given the increasing need for school principals, such an approach would help reduce the shortages of principals in Israeli schools (Husain et al., 2021). The point here is not to discuss the reasons for this shortage, as others have done (Luboshitz, 2018). Rather, under this new plan or model, principalships would be filled, and with mentoring offered along with the preparation course, a closer match between theory and practice would be accomplished.

Another advantage of the new approach is that mentorship would allow the Capstones principal curriculum to be more closely aligned to the individual needs of new principals, whereas in the former model such an alignment was impossible.

Continued research is needed to ascertain the effectiveness of such an effort to provide greater on-the-job support to new principals. Research is needed to study programs that closely coordinate their preparation course with on-the-job mentoring. Extant research in the field of principal preparation (Reed & Kensler, 2010) indicates that such a plan would have several benefits in terms of aiding recruitment to fill the many existing principal vacancies and helping retain these new principals, given the support they would receive via mentoring and induction, briefly discussed below.

MENTORING AND INDUCTION DURING THE EARLY YEARS OF PRINCIPAL LEADERSHIP

The current recruitment and preparation process in Israel first identifies suitable candidates (i.e., those who possess the requisite degrees and teaching experience, which is at least five years). This is followed by the pre-service preparation course (known as the *Course Menhalim* or the Preparation Course for Principals). Then principal candidates obtain their first position after a rigorous interview process and with limited opportunities for mentorship.

As indicated earlier, the disconnect between learning about the theories and practices of school leaders and the ability to apply this knowledge to on-the-job realities is marked. Consequently, under the new model, the Preparation Course for Principals would be offered to only those individuals who are first placed as school principals. This innovation enables the newly designated principal to apply various course teachings to the challenges faced in a real school setting.

While on the job the new principal would be able to apply the principles, content areas, and skill sets learned in the Preparation Course for Principals to their work with the help of a mentor in the school. The role of the mentor is to serve as a support to the principal and to help the newly designated principal to brainstorm ideas as they apply teachings from the Preparation Course for Principals to the challenges they face on the job.

As indicated in the literature (Gentilucci et al., 2013), when new principals (as well as teachers; see Mullen & Fallen, 2022) receive this kind of support, retention rates increase. Recruitment also improves because candidates know in advance that they will receive the support they need to succeed.

Research (e.g., Levin & Bradley, 2019) indicates that principals leave their positions for a variety of reasons. A recent study in Israel highlighted a lack of support in dealing with mandates from the Ministry of Education (i.e., the bureaucracy) (Shenhav et al., 2020). The proposal advocated in this chapter seeks to merge the principal preparation program with the stresses and strains of the first year by allowing principals to learn theory and process actual experience (practice) at the same time, which would allow new principals to understand their role as leader and develop their leadership style.

Of course, the preparation program would not leave principals alone to cope with whatever might befall them on the job. Rather, there would be group and individual mentors affiliated with the course who would work with new principals and guide them through the troubled waters they are liable to encounter in their early careers.

The proposal of this chapter does not seek to change the topics and content of the preparation programs as they exist today. The only change suggested is the self-evident advantage of on-the-job training and mentorship as principals begin their careers. Follow-up research on the value of the mentorship as events unfold in the principal's office should be part of the formative stage of this program, with appropriate adjustments made along the way.

The proposal, however, goes further. With the Preparation Course for Principals now combined with mentorship, the learning and need for support would go beyond the first year. Mentorship, in the form of one-to-one assistance, would occur for two consecutive years (i.e., years one and two), followed by an induction process in the following three years. This induction would be monitored and supported by the Ministry of Education or local officials such as district superintendents.

During induction, principals would engage in meaningfully relevant professional development, not unlike that which has been advocated for teachers. Some activities might include intervisitations, wherein principals are released to visit other schools and principals, and special all-day seminars for principals offered by local university professors on topics selected by the principals themselves, among other activities.

Successful professional development and induction that can lead to enhanced proficiency during the early years of the principalship should be framed by the following components, first outlined by Lieberman (1995; see also Marshall et al., 2022).

- *Purposeful and articulated:* Goals for professional development and induction must be developed, examined, critiqued, and assessed for relevance by principals themselves, in consultation with mentors and/or district or ministry officials. These goals must be stated in some formal way so that all those involved are clear about their intent and purposes.
- *Participatory and collaborative:* Too often professional development programs are top-driven, even at times by administrative fiat. Such programs are less effective because teachers and principals, for whom professional development provides the greatest benefit, are not actively involved in its design, implementation, and assessment. Best practices professional development and induction require participation by all stakeholders.
- *Knowledge-based yet practical:* Professional development must be based on the most relevant and current research in the field. Also, principals will not value professional development unless it is relevant to their lived realities in their schools.
- *Ongoing:* Too much of professional development is of the one-shot variety. If professional development and induction are to make a real difference in the knowledge, skills, and dispositions of principals, then learning opportunities must be provided on a continuous basis so that ideas and practices are sustained.
- *Developmental:* Professional development must not only be ongoing but developmental—it should gradually build on principal knowledge and skills in a given area or topic.
- *Analytical and reflective:* Opportunities for principals to think, articulate, and dialogue with other principals are essential. Principals analyze

their actions in response to challenges they face and with others reflect on ways of solving or at least addressing problems on the job.

IMPLICATIONS FOR RECRUITMENT AND RETENTION OF PRINCIPALS EVERYWHERE

The major contribution of this chapter is its focus on the need to reframe the way we prepare school principals. Neither these ideas nor the situation described in Israel are totally unique, but they do involve some tweaking of existing practices. Both in Israel and other countries, methods of preparing principals rely too heavily on traditional practices and are not always aligned with extant research as well as advocacy in the field of educational leadership.

Three ideas are relevant and urgent: 1) Bridging the gap between theory and practice is axiomatic. 2) Principal preparation needs to be conducted as close as possible to the context in which principals will work and lead. 3) Principals, as with all educators, need ongoing support to gain proficiency in their work and to succeed in the early years of their careers.

The implementation of such a model is likely to improve recruitment to fill principal shortages (Reichel, in press) because prospective principals will realize that their likelihood of success will be much greater with a coherent, well-balanced program. Similarly, retention rates of principals, given the investment into their professional development with both mentoring and induction, will likely increase.

The ideas presented in this chapter can be relevant in many school contexts, even though each district, school, and country has its own organizational, political, economic, and social dynamics. The professional preparation model presented in this chapter proposes that the practical experience of the principal candidate should be carried out during the beginning of their term as an officially appointed principal. In sum, this model has several practical benefits and implications:

- *A richer professional development experience:* This includes a gradual preparation that combines in-depth theoretical studies with genuine field work that is customized to the specific needs of the new principal and is therefore more relevant and significant. The clear implication is that programs that prepare school leaders should ensure a congruity between theory and practice.
- *A more robust on-the-job experience:* There is a more natural connection between the preparation program and the expert mentorship of the principal. This provides the new principal with more support in the early

stages of their career. The implication is to to ensure support early on and for at least the first five years of the new principal's career.
- *A mentorship component is critical:* Programs should be established that ensure structured and ongoing mentorship for all new principals for at least the first two years of their careers.
- *An induction program that includes professional development:* The program should not end with mentoring. Continued support is critical. Taking the principal from a nascent principal aspirant to a bourgeoning professional with a solid base and a forward-looking educational vision takes time and support. Principal induction processes are currently uncommon (Dotres, 2020), yet they are important.

CONCLUSION

Serving as a principal is an awesome responsibility fraught with challenges. The preparation program described, with an example of practices being developed in Israel, is a reminder that principals need support to develop proficiency. Although the implications for recruitment and retention were not fully explored in the limited space of this chapter, the possibilities will be positive given increased support.

REFERENCES

Acker-Hocevar, M., & Cruz-Janzen, M. (2008). Teacher and principal preparation programs: Reforms that sustain high performance and learning in high poverty and diverse schools. *International Journal of Learning, 14*(10), 87–95.

Alsbury, T. L., & Hackmann, D. G. (2006). Learning from experience: Initial findings of a mentoring/induction program for novice principals and superintendents. *Planning and Change, 37*, 169–189.

Bertrand, L. A., Stader, D., & Copeland, S. (2018). Supporting new school leaders through mentoring, *School Leadership Review, 13*(2), 81–94.

Beycioglu, K., & Wildy, H. (2017). Principal preparation: The case of novice principals in Turkey. In K. Beycioglu & P. Pashiardis (Eds.), *Multidimensional perspectives on principal leadership effectiveness* (pp. 1–17). IGI Global.

Brooks, J. S., & Heffernan, A. (Eds.). (2020). *The school leadership survival guide.* Information Age Publishing.

Brown, P. F. (2006). Preparing principals for today's demands. *Phi Delta Kappan, 87*(7), 525–526.

Buzo-Schwartz, M., & Mandel-Levy, N. (2016). The pedagogical leader as a leader of learning processes. In N. Mandel-Levy & M. Buzo-Schwartz (Eds.), *Making a school: Practical knowledge about pedagogical leadership* (pp. 4–9). Avnei Rosha.

Capstones. (2008). *Perception of the principal's role in the State of Israel: Report by the Professional Committee to Formulate Policy Recommendations for the Ministry of Education.* Avney Rosha—The Israel Institute for School Leadership.

Capstones. (2009). *The preparation of school principals in Israel: Report of a professional committee.* Avney Rosha—The Israeli Institute for School Leadership.

Capstones. (2016). *Instructional leadership: Practical points for leadership for active principals in the early stages of their careers and their positions regarding leadership activities.* Avney Rosha—The Israeli Institute for School Leadership [Hebrew].

Capstones. (2021). *The program for the training of school principals for the year 2018.* Avney Rosha—The Israeli Institute for School Leadership.

Cruz-González, C., Rodríguez, C. L., & Segovia, J. D. (2021). A systematic review of principals' leadership identity from 1993 to 2019. *Educational Management Administration & Leadership, 49*(1), 31–53.

Darling-Hammond, L. (2012). Innovative principal preparation programs: What works and how we know. *Planning and Change, 43*(1), 25–46.

Devos, G., & Bouckenooghe, D. (2009). An exploratory study on principals' conceptions about their role as school leaders. *Leadership and Policy in Schools, 8*(2), 173–196.

Dotres, J. L. (2020). *Effective elements of new principal induction programs in large urban school districts.* (Publication No. 27741789) [Doctoral dissertation, St. Thomas University] ProQuest Dissertations & Theses Global.

Forssten-Seiser, A. (2020). Exploring enhanced pedagogical leadership: An action research study involving Swedish principals. *Educational Action Research, 28*(5), 791–806.

Fullan, M. (2001). *The new meaning of educational change (3rd ed.).* Teachers College Press.

Gentilucci, J. L., Denti, L., & Guaglianone, C. L. (2013). New principals' perspectives of their multifaceted role. *Educational Leadership and Administration: Teaching and Program Development, 24*, 75–85.

Gimbel, P., & Kefor, K. (2018). Perceptions of a principal mentoring initiative. *NASSP Bulletin, 102*(1), 22–37.

Glanz, J. (2022). Personal Reflections on supervision as instructional leadership: From whence it came and to where shall it go? *Journal of Educational Supervision, 4*(3). https://doi.org/10.31045/jes.4.3.5

Glickman, C. D., Gordon, S. P., & Ross-Gordon, J. M. (2017). *Supervision and instructional leadership: A developmental approach* (10th ed.). Allyn & Bacon.

Gordon, S. P. (2022). Integrating the experiential learning cycle with educational supervision. *Journal of Educational Supervision, 5*(3). https://doi.org/10.31045/jes.5.3.1

Grissom, J. A., Mitani, H., & Woo, D. S. (2019). Principal preparation programs and principal outcomes. *Educational Administration Quarterly, 55*(1), 73–115.

Hess, F. M., & Kelly, A. P. (2007). Learning to lead: What gets taught in principal preparation programs. *Teachers College Record, 109*(1), 244–274.

Hurst, J. (2021). *What do principals do?* Information Age Publishing.

Husain, A. N., Miller, L. Luke, C., & Player, D. W. (2021). Quality to understand who leaves the principalship. *Educational Administration Quarterly, 57*(5), 683–715.

Hussain, S. T., Akram, T., & Haider, M. J. (2018). Kurt Lewin's change model: A critical review of the role of leadership and employee involvement in organizational change. *Journal of Innovation & Knowledge, 3*(3), 123–127.

Israeli Central Bureau of Statistics. (2013). *Statistical Abstract of Israel* (No. 64).

Levin, S., & Bradley, K. (2019). Understanding and addressing principal turnover: A review of the research. *Learning Policy Institute, National Association of Secondary School Principals.* https://learningpolicyinstitute.org/media/326/download?inline&file=NASSP_LPI_Principal_Turnover_Research_Review_REPORT.pdf

Lieberman, A. (1995). *The work of restructuring schools: Building from the ground up.* Teachers College Press.

Luboshitz, Z. (2018). Appointment of administrators in the education system. *Policy Paper, 38,* Kohelet Policy Forum [Hebrew]. https://kohelet.org.il/wp-content/uploads/2018/07/KPF082_Appointing-educational-principals_ELECTRONIC_300718.pdf

Lynch, J. M. (2012). Responsibilities of today's principal: Implications for principal preparation programs and principal certification policies. *Rural Special Education Quarterly, 31*(2), 40–47.

Male, T., & Palaiologou, I. (2012). Learning-centered leadership or pedagogical leadership? An alternative approach to leadership in educational contexts. *International Journal of Leadership in Education, 15*(1), 107–118.

Marshall, I., Jackman, G. A., & Armstrong, D. E. (Eds.). (2022). *The early years of leadership: The journey begins.* Information Age Publishing.

Mullen, C., & Fallen, M. (2022). Navigating uncharted waters: New teacher mentoring and induction. *Research in Educational Administration and Leadership, 7*(4), 751–785.

Murphy, M. (2019). *Leadership styles.* Leadership IQ Press.

Nasser-Abu Alhija, F., & Fresko, B. (2014). An exploration of the relationships between mentor recruitment, the implementation of mentoring, and mentors' attitudes. *Mentoring & Tutoring: Partnership in Learning, 22*(2), 162–180.

New Leaders. (2012). *Improving principal preparation: A review of current practices.* https://www.ncsl.org/Portals/1/Documents/educ/TP_Prep_PrincipalPreparationNewLeaders.pdf

Pannell, S., Peltier-Glaze, B., Haynes, I., & Skelton, C. (2015). Evaluating the effectiveness of traditional and alternative principal preparation programs. *Journal of Organizational & Educational Leadership, 1*(2), http://digitalcommons.gardner-webb.edu/joel/vol1/iss2/3

Reed, C. J., & Kensler, L. A. W. (2010). Creating a new system for principal preparation: Reflections on efforts to transcend tradition and create new cultures. *Journal of Research on Leadership Education, 5*(12), 568–582.

Reichel, M. (in press). Towards a solution to solve the shortage of principals in Israel by recruiting Anglo former principals. In C. Rabinowitz & M. Reichel, (Eds.),

Principal recruitment and retention: Best practices for meeting the challenges today. Rowman & Littlefield.

Roegman, R., & Woulfin, S. (2019). Reconceptualizing the nature of the theory-practice gap in K–12 educational leadership. *Journal of Educational Administration, 57*(1), 2–20.

Schon, D. (1992/2017). *The reflective practitioner: How professionals think in action.* Basic Books.

Shahaf, G., Katz, T., Yaakovzon, Y., & Fisher, S. (2011). Avney Rosha—The Israeli Institute for School Leadership.

Shaked, H. (published online 2021, in press). Relationship-based instructional leadership. *International Journal of Leadership in Education.* https://doi.org/10.1080/13603124.2021.1944673

Shaked, H. (2022). *New explorations for instructional leaders: How principals promote teaching and learning.* Rowman & Littlefield.

Shenhav S., Geffon A., Salomon L., & Glanz, J. (2020). Encouraging and discouraging factors in the decision to become an Israeli leader in religious schools: Implications for reforming bureaucratic mandates of the Ministry of Education. *International Journal of Educational Reform, 30*(1), 77–97.

Slater, C. L., & Nelson, S. W. (2013). *Understanding the principalship: An international guide.* Emerald.

Villiani, S. (2014). *Mentoring and induction that support new principals.* Corwin.

Wasonga, T. A., & Murphy, J. F. (2006). Learning from tacit knowledge: The impact of the internship. *International Journal of Educational Management, 20*(6), 226–287.

Wilmore, E. L. (2004). *Principal induction: A standards-based model for administrator development.* Corwin.

Zepeda, S. J. (Ed.). (2008). *Real world supervision: Adapting theory to practice.* Rowman & Littlefield.

Chapter 10

A Proposal to Enhance Retention of School Principals in Türkiye

Pınar Ayyıldız, Ankara Medipol University
Köksal Banoğlu, Turkish Ministry
of National Education

Principal retention has been a growing concern around the globe, since school principals are in a unique position with their hard-earned and thus vital managerial experience, which allows them to have a fine-grained understanding of schools (Gunraj & Rutherford, 1999). A principal's decision to quit or stay at their current school is heavily influenced by both school-related working conditions and policy-driven contextual factors (Yan, 2020).

The loss of an ideal equilibrium between the school and policy results in principal turnover, which is likely to be disruptive to the school climate and eventually to school improvement (Hanselman et al., 2016). As a result, it is evident that a change of the school manager can be a key change for the whole school (Pietsch et al., 2020). Research has also consistently demonstrated that "despite the importance of school leaders, the ability to retain quality principals has proven to be a substantial challenge" (Mandel & Pendola, 2021, p. 3).

In this chapter, we scrutinize central issues pertaining to principal retention in the context of Türkiye's highly centralized educational system, which does not allow for school autonomy. Afterwards, we shall review individual and societal consequences of principal turnover to better identify underlying systemic concerns. With this in mind, we concentrate on the following question: What needs to be done to maintain successful principals in Turkish schools?

To answer this question, we seek to gain insight into the circumstances and settings in Türkiye, which will enable us to develop a new model and hopefully reverse the turnover trend. Perhaps, with this model, we will illuminate ways to not only reverse the trend in our home country, but to also offer help to other countries facing the same turnover conundrum. The positive retention of successful principals around the world will be our measure of success. Using the Turkish context can be especially edifying for researchers around the world as we keep Slater et al. (2018, p. 127) in mind: "Research on school leadership hardly extended outside of Anglo-Saxon countries and a handful of other European counterparts until the past decade."

THEORETICAL UNDERPINNINGS

The major concepts of principal retention are defined in this section, along with potential opportunities and risks facing Türkiye and, to some extent, the world as a whole. We will also reframe the conceptual bases for principal retention with a dialectical viewpoint conceptualizes *attrition* and *turnover* as the polar opposites of the notion of *retention*.

Given this perspective, we draw on a list of underlying causes of principal turnover, as proposed by Levin and Bradley (2019, p. 3): "inadequate preparation and professional development, poor working conditions, insufficient salaries, lack of decision-making authority, [and] high-stakes accountability policies." In response to these gaps, we issue a call for improvements in principal preparation and professional development programs, as well as better working conditions and proper compensation.

Business and school management scholarship have long engaged in a heated debate over the issue of whether leaders are born or created. It is intriguing to consider whether school administrators are in fact principals from the very beginning of their careers or whether they are later shaped to fill that role over the course of their careers.

Several past studies inquired about the elements of emerging principal agency, or more structurally, the pipeline to the principalship (Bartanen et. al., 2020), which affects a person's choice to become a principal (Farley-Ripple et al., 2012; Myung et al., 2011; Parylo et al., 2013). To fully understand multiple facets of the issue, it is crucial to grasp what motivates school administrators to shoulder the burden of leadership, be it wholeheartedly or hesitantly (Szczesiul & Huizenga, 2014).

Given the potential trade-offs involved in a school principal's decision to stay in or leave the profession, one might think it is a rational choice that is made individually at some point in each principals' career. However, there is a growing and convincing body of evidence that principal leave is more than merely a personal choice (e.g., Akiba & Reichardt, 2004; Tekleselassie & Villarreal, 2011; Yan, 2020).

A principal's choice to remain at their current school for an extended period of time—commonly known as principal retention—is not determined by the passage of time (Snodgrass Rangel, 2017). This is primarily because school management is operationalized within nested ecological systems comprised of school, district, and policy-level parameters that may all impact the school environment as well as individual actions (Beckett, 2018).

Scholars and practitioners are always looking for research-based ways to improve educational policies regarding principal retention. Principals are often compensated based on criteria such as type of school, difficulties of the job, needs of the students, and size of the operation undertaken. Their job descriptions should be written according to the same criteria. This is a more just way of judging principal performance and their retention (Pijanowski et al., 2009). Once a principal's job description and expectations are clearly established, the likely negative effects of principal turnover due to poor performance may be justified.

Conversely, without clear expectations of the role, the school community may suffer the adverse effects of principal turnover. The departure of a principal might have a far more negative impact on the school when a less qualified successor is appointed (Bartanen et al., 2019). Accordingly, it is clear that there exist multifaceted negative consequences of principal attrition that affect students, teachers, and other school stakeholders; therefore, there is a need to better understand the intricacies of principal retention.

At the policy level, the degree of school autonomy versus district centralization in management systems is of direct relevance to the nature of the policy instruments in use. Vesely (2012) distinguishes four fundamental classes of policy instruments that influence principal and teacher behaviors, such as regulatory instruments (laws and regulations), economic instruments (incentives and sanctions), information instruments (campaigns and training programs), and monitoring and evaluation instruments (nationwide tests and curriculum requirements). Although educational policymakers tend to endorse information instruments (such as in-service days or professional development programs) to be more effective (Vesely & Petrusek, 2020), school principals have mostly preferred the regulatory and economic instruments in their decision-making (Papa, 2007).

Further, district policies differ between countries due to the different legislatures that govern them (White & Cooper, 2011). Nevertheless, scholars (e.g., Burkhauser, 2017; Cannata et al., 2017; Kraft et al., 2016) contend that while principals work to improve their own schools' cultures and gain adherents to their cause, they may or may not have a significant and direct impact on student learning and accomplishment. Thence, informed discussions regarding principal retention must be conducted within both the national and local contexts, making educational policy ever-changing and sometimes overly hermeneutical (Oplatka, 2011).

Norton (2003) reminds us that a principal's main task is to improve instruction and learning. However, so many constraints prevent them from accomplishing this paramount task. Accountability, a high workload, workplace stress, and ever-changing legal responsibilities all contribute to rising turnover and a shortage of qualified replacements (National Conference of State Legislatures, 2002).

Subsequently, Wang et al. (2021) adds job intensification and the absence of job satisfaction to the previous constraints. To some extent, all these components may act individually or in combination to cause principal turnover. We shall now focus on the principal retention issue within extremely centralized education systems that are usually characterized by low levels of school autonomy.

HISTORICAL BACKGROUND OF PRINCIPAL APPOINTMENT AND RETENTION POLICIES IN TÜRKIYE

This section sheds light on the relevant legislation in Türkiye. Over the past two decades, the Turkish education system has experienced unsustainable state-centered school reform initiatives (Sezer, 2016). As a matter of fact, administrative education staff policies in Türkiye have been subject to numerous regulatory revisions that govern tenure, promotion, and reappointment processes in public schools (Aydın-Baş & Şentürk, 2017).

Nevertheless, an expanding and convincing body of research suggests that any school reform initiative is reliant on the principal's efforts to build a commonly shared school vision that focuses on implementing the reform agenda over several years (Balyer & Gündüz, 2011; Logan, 2017; Taylor-Pearce et al., 2021). How principals succeed at implementing that reform agenda depends on why they have entered the principalship and how long they are entitled to pursue their professional career goals within a given policy context (Beycioğlu & Wildy, 2015; Wildy & Clarke, 2008).

School management has never been deemed a certified or legitimate profession in Türkiye. Instead, it has typically meant the promotion of the most "proper" teacher to the vacant administrative position (Bursalıoğlu, 2005). Indeed, successful classroom teachers cannot guarantee their success in the principalship (Işık, 2003). Until 2009, Turkish school principals, once appointed, would continue to work at the same school for as long as they wished, and switched to other schools only if they wanted to do so (Şimşek, 2013).

Following an amendment to the articles of School Principals' Appointment and Reappointment Regulation in 2009, a principal rotation system was put into practice. By this legislative adjustment, principal tenure in a public school was limited to a period of five years at the same school.

An amendment that came into effect in 2014 reduced principal tenure from five to four years within the same school, allowing for a four-year-long reappointment to another school. Reappointment for successive terms was made conditional on passing oral and written examination at 75% proficiency. The oral examination board has always been made up of provincial and district superintendents who are accountable to governmental bodies, including the Ministry of Interior Affairs for administrative tasks and the Ministry of Education for educational responsibilities.

The written exam preparation committee remained likewise subservient to central governmental bodies headed by the minister from the ruling political party. Specific articles regulating the appointment standards established through oral interviews and government-approved achievement certificates were severely challenged by teacher unions and, consequently, amended twice in 2013 and once every year from 2014 to 2018.

After each of these adjustments, nepotism debates resurfaced as the key provisions failed to establish objective criteria for the reappointment of school principals (Beycioğlu et al., 2018). Consequently, scores of inexperienced principals were placed in schools, whereas senior fellows were not reappointed (Kılınç et al., 2021). As a result, the reliability of unstructured interviews became questionable in the highly centralized Turkish education system, and the reappointment agency was extensively criticized for being arbitrary (Akbaşlı et al, 2017).

Newly appointed principals have often been accused of having ties to the authorities and being partisans owing to the huge effect of power struggles and government-led unions on the recruitment and reappointment processes (Beycioğlu et al., 2018; Kondakçı et al., 2019). These factors have created a built-in discontinuity to administrative staff policies, bred unprofessionalism in schools, and undermined principal retention.

AN URGENT NEED TO ACT

This section discusses reasons for taking action that is feasible and sustainable for Türkiye and is also sensitive to the changing dynamics of the educational "biosphere" in our country. A biosphere is defined as a nonorganic construction with one or more self-contained ecosystems. We believe that this definition, together with the scholarly work of Bronfenbrenner (1979), sheds light on the inspirational words of Turan (2000, p. 544): "understanding society and its interrelation with schools has long been ignored by educational reformers and leaders. Educational reforms and studies have directed attention to the school and ignored its relationship with the different dimensions of social, political, and economic life."

We use *biosphere* as a metaphor here, since it echoes the sophisticated and dynamic nature of the principalship. We find this metaphor to be particularly apt if we take a bird's eye view and see the interconnected and symbiotic relationships between the education system and other societal systems in a holistic manner.

To better understand the concepts of *configuration* and *holistic*, it might be helpful to resituate them within the schema of the principalship. To begin with configuration, recall that the principalship is made up of visible and invisible components, such as the principal as an individual, the roles and responsibilities that the position entails, and the relationships between and among the members of the school and other stakeholders. To locate the principalship in a holistic context, one must see all of these elements as part of the configuration, and acknowledge that the principalship necessitates an integrated outlook.

As the research literature has proven, and as practice has indicated, there is more than one factor that makes the principalship successful, and principals must be cognizant of these factors throughout their careers. These factors include the principal's personal characteristics such as levels of readiness and motivation as well as leadership abilities; organizational characteristics such as the school ethos, values, culture, and climate, and policy-based factors such as the laws and multifarious decisions made by elected and professional leaders.

A visual representation of a typical biosphere of the principalship in Türkiye is represented below. Figure 10.1 represents these elements in relation to principal retention. Concurrently, we note both the shifts at the regional and global levels (e.g., the recent pandemic and financial stagnation) and the paradigm shifts occurring over the longer run. These consistently impact local biospheres.

Figure 10.1 hints at the fact that principal retention constitutes an interconnected circle with three parts: the principal as a human being, schools as institutional entities, and the policies involved. One way to assure principal retention is by considering principals' needs, expectations, and desires. These may be supported by members of the larger school community, namely board members and other educational policymakers, as they reach macro-level decisions that ultimately help principals with their personal development.

Thus, when the lay leadership responds well to the principal's personal needs, they ensure the principal's well-being and enhance principal retention. By this means, they may also prevent principal burnout. Friedman (1995)

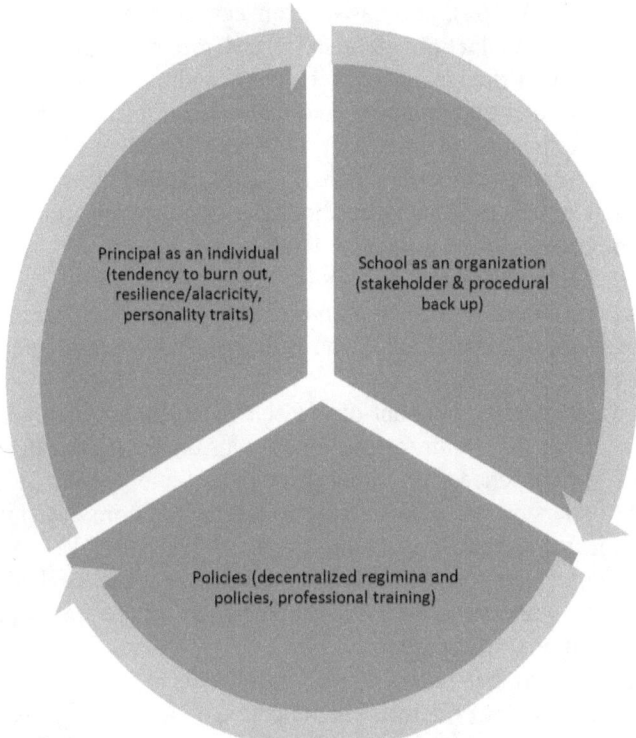

Figure 10.1. The Biosphere of the School Principalship in Relation to Retention

defines burnout as "emotional, cognitive and physical exhaustion and weariness, aloofness, self-dissatisfaction and discontent, and also deprecation and distrust in staff" (p. 193). More recently, feelings of incompetency, lower motivation levels, and general feelings of being stressed out have been added to the list (Karaköse et al., 2016).

When a principal's retention is at risk, peer coaching serves as the best solution to inspire a collective commitment throughout the educational district and to help individual principals preserve their positions in schools. Principals can share their stories, learn together, sympathize with each other, and understand each other's vulnerabilities and challenges. One method of enhancing communication is the exchange of diaries among the principals. Each leader records the highlights and challenges of the position. These are then discussed and reacted to in a safe and supportive environment.

The school as an organization is the second component of our school biosphere. This component includes the presence and roles of existing groups and their leaders within the school. According to Hulpia and Devos (2009), the second component is "the strongest predictor of school leaders' job satisfaction" (p. 163). Job satisfaction can ensure principal retention. Assuring the job satisfaction of other school groups is also important to principal retention. Principals need to create situations in which the relevant groups are allowed to take initiative and make decisions that matter.

This empowerment of others reflects well on principals and increases their job ratings by others (Short & Rinehart, 1992). Şahin (2018) clarified that empowerment of others is not just about the principal creating better situations for others as part of a decentralization plan. It also allows principals to maintain their own mental well-being by delegating tasks. Elected and professional leaders must also be mindful of the worries, expectations, and recommendations of the principal, who is uniquely situated to be heeded and accommodated.

The third and final component of our school biosphere includes national and local policies that confront the innate tension between autonomy and accountability experienced by school principals (Steinberg 2013). This tension can be understood as a conflict between having more decision-making autonomy and being held accountable for these decisions. We acknowledge that, to a certain extent, centralization is indispensable, yet local adjustments still need to be made to ensure that judgments of school performance are obtained in a fair and transparent manner.

That being said, in the Turkish context individuals in middle-level management positions (such as principals) are encouraged to turn to others who are recognized as the ones "who knows things better" (Aydoğdu & Sever, 2020). It is worth reiterating that the necessity and value of the principalship as a profession should be matched with the concomitant appropriate salaries and employee benefits.

In addition, as a matter of legislated policy, professionally planned and executed pre-service and in-service staff development sessions must be available for school leaders everywhere in Türkiye. Our Turkish principals come from various and colorful backgrounds. They bring a myriad of talents to their chosen profession. They are qualified and capable of leading schools that cater to many types of students, parents, and communities. But professional development will aid them in honing their skills and perfecting their inherent talents.

We suggest that these sessions be part of graduate courses, conferences, and workshops. Staff development can also take place in the form of individual or small-group mentoring. The leaders of such events should be recognized educationalists (i.e., academics and other experts). Alternately, experienced principals should be hired to plan and present peer learning sessions to their less-experienced colleagues. Their wisdom will surely enrich the next generation of educational leaders.

CONCLUSION

Studies conducted in Türkiye on principal retention (e.g., Bayar, 2016) found that early career principals are particularly susceptible to discouragement. Many leave the profession with little hope of return. We encourage these perplexed men and women to be patient and steadfast in their career choice. For research suggests (e.g., Wahlstrom et. al, 2010) that when principals stay at a school for at least five years, they can directly and indirectly improve recruitment, retention, and staff capacity building.

Nonetheless, school leadership positions are so complex and intricate that we advise novice and seasoned principals alike to search for professional support and development. If the school is understood as part of a larger biosphere, school principals should find or create healthy avenues of communication and cooperation with people and also with institutions both in and outside the school. Accordingly, we are of the same opinion as Cieminski (2015) that retention is a matter of preparing, recruiting, and selecting leaders and then socializing, onboarding, and inducting these individuals.

REFERENCES

Akbaşlı, S., Şahin, M., & Gül, B. (2017). Selection process of school principals in Turkey and some other countries: A comparative study. *Universal Journal of Educational Research, 5*(12), 2251–2258.

Akiba, M., & Reichardt, R. (2004). What predicts the mobility of elementary school leaders? An analysis of longitudinal data in Colorado. *Education Policy Analysis Archives, 12*, 18.

Aydın-Baş, E., & Şentürk, İ. (2017). Eğitim kurumları yöneticilerinin görevlendirilmelerine ilişkin yönetmelik hakkında okul yöneticilerinin görüşleri [Opinions of school administrators about the regulation of appointments of administrators of educational institutions]. *Ondokuz Mayıs Üniversitesi Eğitim Fakültesi Dergisi, 36*(2), 119–143.

Aydoğdu, E., & Sever, M. (2020). Principalship in building shared meanings in school. *Kuram Ve Uygulamada Eğitim Yönetimi, 26*(1), 59–116. https://www.kuey.net/index.php/kuey/article/view/8

Balyer, A., & Gündüz, Y. (2011). Değişik ülkelerde okul müdürlerinin yetiştirilmesi: Türk eğitim sistemi için bir model önerisi [Training of school principals in different countries: A model proposal for the Turkish education system]. *Kuramsal Eğitimbilim, 4*(2), 182–197.

Bartanen, B., Grissom, J. A., & Rogers, L. K. (2019). The impacts of principal turnover. *Educational Evaluation and Policy Analysis, 41*(3), 350–374.

Bartanen, B., Rogers, L. K., & Woo, D. S. (2020). *Assistant principal mobility and its relationship with principal turnover* (EdWorkingPaper No. 20–275). Annenberg Institute at Brown University. https://doi.org/10.26300/jx8g-qq97

Bayar, A. (2016). Challenges facing principals in the first year at their schools. *Universal Journal of Educational Research*, 4(1), 192–199.

Beckett, L. O. (2018). Predictors of urban principal turnover. *Urban Education*, 56(10), 1695–1718.

Beycioglu, K., & Wildy, H. (2015). Principal preparation: The case of novice principals in Turkey. In K. Beycioglu & P. Pashiardis (Eds.), *Multidimensional perspectives on principal leadership effectiveness* (pp. 1–17). IGI Global.

Beycioğlu, K., Şahin, I., & Kesik, F. (2018). Analysis of maladministration of selection and assignment of school principals in Turkey: A critical perspective. In E. Samier & P. Milley (Eds.), *International perspectives on maladministration in education* (pp.137–150). Routledge.

Bronfenbrenner, U. (1979). *The ecology of human development: Experiments by nature and design*. Harvard University Press.

Burkhauser, S. (2017). How much do school principals matter when it comes to teacher working conditions? *Educational Evaluation and Policy Analysis*, 39(1), 126–145.

Bursalıoğlu, Z. (2005). *Eğitim yönetiminde teori ve uygulama* [Theory and practice in educational administration]. Pegem A Yayıncılık.

Cannata, M., Rubin, M., Goldring, E., Grissom, J. A., Neumerski, C. M., Drake, T. A., & Schuermann, P. (2017). Using teacher effectiveness data for information-rich hiring. *Educational Administration Quarterly*, 53(2), 180–222.

Cieminski, A. B. (2015). *Practices that support principal succession* [Unpublished doctoral dissertation]. University of Northern Colorado.

Farley-Ripple, E. N., Raffel, J. A., & Welch, J. C. (2012). Administrator career paths and decision processes. *Journal of Educational Administration*, 50(6), 788–816.

Friedman, I. A. (1995). School principal burnout: The concept and its components. *Journal of Organizational Behavior*, 16(2), 191–198.

Gunraj, J., & Rutherford, D. (1999). A preliminary evaluation of HEADLAMP Programme for newly appointed headteachers. *Educational Management & Administration*, 27(2), 143–154.

Hanselman, P., Grigg, J., Bruch, S. K., & Gamoran, A. (2016). The consequences of principal and teacher turnover for school social resources. *Family Environments, School Resources, and Educational Outcomes*, 19, 49–89.

Hulpia, H., & Devos, G. (2009). Exploring the link between distributed leadership and job satisfaction of school leaders. *Educational Studies*, 35(2), 153–171.

Işık, H. (2003). From policy into practice: The effects of principal preparation programs on principal behavior. *International Journal of Educational Reform*, 12(4), 260–274.

Karaköse, T., Kocabas, I., Yirci, R., Esen, C., & Celik, M. (2016). Exploring the relationship between school principals' burnout situation and life satisfaction. *Universal Journal of Educational Research*, 4(6), 1488–1494.

Kılınç, A., Er, E., & Beycioğlu, K. (2021). Mapping the terrain of training and appointment of educational leaders in the Turkish context: An historical perspective. In E. A. Samier, E. S. Elkaleh, & W. Hammad (Eds.), *Internationalisation of educational administration and leadership curriculum* (pp. 139–157). Emerald Publishing.

Kondakci, Y., Orucu, D., Oguz, E., & Beycioglu, K. (2019). Large-scale change and survival of school principals in Turkey. *Journal of Educational Administration and History, 51*(4), 301–315. https://doi.org/10.1080/00220620.2019.1574724

Kraft, M. A., Marinell, W. H., & Shen-Wei Yee, D. (2016). School organizational contexts, teacher turnover, and student achievement: Evidence from panel data. *American Educational Research Journal, 53*(5), 1411–1449.

Levin, S., & Bradley, K. (2019). *Understanding and addressing principal turnover: A review of the research* (EdWorkingPaper No. 19–179). Annenberg Institute at Brown University. https://www.edworkingpapers.com/ai19-179

Logan, C. J. (2017). *The leadership practices of successful urban elementary school principals and their roots.* (Publication No. 10265435) [Doctoral dissertation, University of Pennsylvania]. ProQuest Dissertations & Theses Global.

Mandel, Z., & Pendola, A. (2021). Policy and principal turnover: The impact of the Texas special education cap. *Education Policy Analysis Archives, 29*(152). https://doi.org/10.14507/epaa.29.5681

Myung, J., Loeb, S., & Horng, E. (2011). Tapping the principal pipeline: Identifying talent for future school leadership in the absence of formal succession management programs. *Educational Administration Quarterly, 47*(5), 695–727.

National Conference of State Legislatures. (2002). *The role of school leadership in improving student achievement.* (ERIC No. ED479288). https://files.eric.ed.gov/fulltext/ED479288.pdf

Norton, M. S. (2003). Let's keep our quality school principals on the job. *The High School Journal, 86*(2), 50–56.

Oplatka, I. (2011). Epilogue. In R. F. White & K. Cooper (Eds), *Principals in succession: Transfer and rotation in educational administration* (pp. 157–168). Routledge.

Papa, F. (2007). Why do principals change schools? A multivariate analysis of principal retention. *Leadership and Policy in Schools, 6*, 267–290.

Parylo, O., Zepeda, S. J., & Bengtson, E. (2013). The different faces of principal mentorship. *International Journal of Mentoring and Coaching in Education, 1*(2), 120–135.

Pietsch, M., Tulowitzki, P., & Hartig, J. (2020) Examining the effect of principal turnover on teaching quality: A study on organizational change with repeated classroom observations. *School Effectiveness and School Improvement, 31*(3), 333–355.

Pijanowski, J. C., Hewitt, P. M., & Brady, K. P. (2009). Superintendents' perceptions of the principal shortage. *National Association of Secondary School Principals Bulletin, 93*(2), 85–95.

Şahin, A. (2018). The opinions of school principals on decentralization in education. *Turkish Journal of Education, 7*(2), 55–85.

Sezer, Ş. (2016). School administrators' opinions on frequently changing regulations related to appointments and relocation: A new model proposal. *Educational Sciences: Theory & Practice, 16*(2), 335–356.

Short, P. M., & Rinehart, J. S. (1992). *Teacher empowerment and school climate* [Paper presentation]. Annual Meeting of the American Educational Research Association. San Francisco, CA.

Şimşek, E. (2013). İstanbul ilindeki resmi okul ve kurum müdürlerinin 2001–2011 yılları arasındaki yer değiştirme sıklıkları üzerine bir araştırma [Research on the frequency of relocation of official school and institution principals in Istanbul, 2001–2011]. *Hasan Ali Yücel Eğitim Fakültesi Dergisi, 19*, 91–103.

Slater, C. L., Garcia Garduno, J. M., & Mentz, K. (2018). Frameworks for principal preparation and leadership development: Contributions of the International Study of Principal Preparation (ISPP). *Management in Education, 32*(3), 126–134.

Snodgrass Rangel, V. (2017). A review of the literature on principal turnover. *Review of Educational Research, 88*(1), 87–124.

Steinberg, M. P. (2013). *Leadership and the decentralized control of schools*. Regional Educational Laboratory Mid-Atlantic. (ERIC No. ED557946). https://files.eric.ed.gov/fulltext/ED557946.pdf

Szczesiul, S., & Huizenga, J. (2014). The burden of leadership: Exploring the principal's role in teacher collaboration. *Improving Schools, 17*(2), 176–191.

Taylor-Pearce, M., Carrol, B., & Bindi, G. (2021). School principals making sense of a national reform agenda: The case of Sierra Leone. *International Journal of Leadership in Education*. Advance online publication. https://doi.org/10.1080/13603124.2021.1889684

Tekleselassie, A. A., & Villarreal, P. (2011). Career mobility and departure intentions among school principals in the United States: Incentives and disincentives. *Leadership and Policy in Schools, 10*(3), 251–293.

Turan, S. (2000). John Dewey's report of 1924 and his recommendations on the Turkish educational system revisited. *History of Education, 29*(6), 543–555.

Vesely, A. (2012). A conceptual framework for comparison of educational policies. *KEDI Journal of Education Policy, 9*(2), 323–347.

Vesely, A., & Petrusek, I. (2020). Decision makers' preferences of policy instruments. *European Policy Analysis, 7*(1), 165–184.

Wahlstrom, K., Louis, K., Leithwood, K., & Anderson, S. (2010). *Learning from leadership: Investigating the links to improved student learning*. The Wallace Foundation. https://www.wallacefoundation.org/knowledge-center/Documents/Investigating-the-Links-to-Improved-Student-Learning.pdf

Wang, F., Hauseman, C., & Pollock, K. (2021). "I am here for the students": Principals' perception of accountability amid work intensification. *Educational Assessment, Evaluation and Accountability, 34*, 1–24.

White, R. E., & Cooper, K. (2011). Introduction. In R. F. White & K. Cooper (Eds.), *Principals in succession: Transfer and rotation in educational administration* (p. 16). Routledge.

Wildy, H., & Clarke, S. (2008). Principals on L-plates: Rear view mirror reflections. *Journal of Educational Administration, 46,* 727–738.

Yan, R. (2020). The influence of working conditions on principal turnover in K–12 public schools. *Educational Administration Quarterly, 56*(1), 89–122.

Index

assistant principal, 10, 34–37, 46, 61–62, 76, 101

BIPOC and diversity, 57, 65; explicit biases against hiring, 60, 62–63, 64; gender bias, 22; implicit biases against hiring, 60, 64; student outcomes, 59

distributed (shared) leadership, 76–77

institutional churn, 69, 70, 80
instructional leadership, 99, 112; chilling effect on principal recruitment, 91–92; definition and conceptualization, 85–89; disinterest in becoming principals, 86; accountability for student outcomes, 85–86, 98, 101–2, 104, 106; four dimensions, 87–88; importance among principals, 88–91. *See also* principal recruitment difficulties
Israeli school system, 31–32, 37, 113

leadership, 43–53, 59, 62–64, 97, 99, 102–3, 106
Leadership Preparation Program (LPP), 45–53

mentoring and induction, 38, 60, 79; 131, 133

New Zealand's national education system: background of the education system, 18–19; Selwyn College model, 23; Tomorrow's Schools reform, 18–19, 29–30. *See also* New Zealand's national education system, board of trustees and governance
New Zealand's national education system, board of trustees and governance, 17, 19–21, 29; lack of experience of the school boards, 23–24; support mechanisms of BOTs, 24–25

parental involvement, 77
Powerful Learning Experiences (PLEs), 47–52
principal pre-service orientation 32, 37, 46–47, 116
principal recruitment: difficulties of finding suitable candidates, 2–3, 31–34, 39, 59–61, 63, 120; geographic limitations and solutions, 60–61, 64–65; New Zealand approach and its challenges, 21, 24–25; programs to remedy shortage

of candidates, 4–8, 9–11, 26–27, 33, 36, 39, 48–50, 62–65; reticence of teachers with instructional expertise to become principals, 91–93; succession planning, 3–5, 77–79

principal retention, 118, 120; and student achievement, 70, 85, 97, 132; job satisfaction, 50, 74–75, 132; turnover and attrition, 44, 45, 53, 69–70, 71–2, 80, 97–99, 126–27; practices to retain principals, 72; work-family conflict, 74–75. *See also* principal retention practices

principal retention practices 72; adequate compensation, 45, 73; authority to make decisions, 73, 76, 127–28; sense of achievement, 75–76; tenure, 73; working conditions, 72

principal-teacher relationships, 48–52, 76, 104–06

racial diversity, 58–59, 62–63
rural schools, 48–50, 57, 60–62, 64–65

support of school district/ministry of education, 24–26, 39, 52

Türkiye's educational system, 125, 127; biosphere and the Turkish context, 129–33; ecological systems that impact on principals' decisions, 127, 129–30; nepotism, 129; principal empowerment and professional development, 129, 132; school autonomy, 127; school reform, 128

About the Editors and Contributors

Chanina A. Rabinowitz served as a school principal on three continents. He received his doctorate in school leadership and policy studies from Loyola University of Chicago. He taught graduate students at Michlalah College, Jerusalem, and English at a public high school there. He now directs and teaches a teacher training program at The Hebrew University of Jerusalem. Email: drchanina@gmail.com

Michael Reichel is an adjunct professor in the Leadership and Management of Educational Systems program at Michlalah Jerusalem College and Orot College. He was a school administrator in Jewish elementary and middle schools for over twenty years in the United States as well as Jerusalem, Israel. His research interests include management leadership, theories of educational administration, bridging theory with practice in educational administration programs, and recruitment strategies for hiring qualified principals. He is also an ordained Orthodox rabbi and has published a manuscript on Persian American Jews. Email: rmreichel@hotmail.com

* * *

Pınar Ayyıldız is an interpreter, sociologist, and teacher trainer, and holds master's and doctorate degrees in educational management as well as a Cambridge Diploma in Teaching English to Speakers of Other Languages (DELTA). She also acted as a DELTA trainer. She has worked as a head teacher and director of an English preparatory school and as an academic coordinator and dean of students in several higher education institutions. To date she has taught numerous courses at the university level. She concentrates on topics including the epistemology of educational sciences, equity in education, and educational leadership. She has many academic memberships and is the editor of international journals including *Participatory Educational Research* (*PER*) and the *Philosophy and Theory in Higher Education Journal*

(*PTHE*). She is currently an associate professor and coordinator of instructional processes in the Management Information Systems Department at Ankara Medipol University in Türkiye. Email: pinarayyildiz@yahoo.com

Köksal Banoğlu received a doctorate in educational sciences from Ghent University and a doctorate in educational management and supervision from Marmara University. He taught graduate and undergraduate courses in various universities in Istanbul, Turkey. Some of his research interests are technology leadership, organizational learning, school health, and applied statistics. His more recent research is on applying probabilistic/inferential social network analysis (SNA) approaches to the investigation of school principals' technology leadership practices, teachers' professional learning interactions, and children's peer aggression/bullying behaviors in school settings. Email: koksal_banoglu@hotmail.com

David G. Buckman is an associate dean and associate professor of educational leadership at Augusta University in Augusta, Georgia. He studies human resources and finance issues in the P–12 educational environment and is the editorial board chair of the *Journal of Education Human Resources* (*JEHR*). Email: dbuckman@augusta.edu

Kathleen M. W. Cunningham is an assistant professor in the Department of Educational Leadership and Policies at the University of South Carolina. Her research centers on educational leadership and includes the areas of leadership preparation programs, improvement science, and the intersection of science education with policy and leadership. Email: katiemwc@mailbox.sc.edu

Gülay Erin Dalgıç is a lecturer and academic developer at the University of Auckland, Faculty of Medical and Health Sciences. She has conducted educational leadership research in the United States, Denmark, Turkey, and New Zealand. Her research interests include principals as reflective practitioners, technology leadership, curriculum development, and e-Assessment in higher education. She has published in journals such as *Teachers and Teaching: Theory and Practice*, the *International Journal of Mentoring and Coaching in Education*, and *Professional Development in Education*. She is an active member of the Australian Association for Research in Education Society. Email: g.dalgic@auckland.ac.nz

Simone A. F. Gause is an assistant professor in the Department of Education Sciences and Organizations at Coastal Carolina University. She earned her PhD in educational administration in 2016 from the University of South Carolina. Her primary scholarly interest is issues of privilege and power and how they impact gender equity, racial equity, and leadership diversity in educational settings. Specifically, her research examines the continued disproportionality and intersectionality of race and gender in educational leadership through historical and contemporary contexts, the experiences of marginalized students and faculty in higher education, faculty diversity, and mentorship. Email: sgause1@coastal.edu

Belinda Gimbert is an associate professor of educational administration in the Department of Educational Studies at The Ohio State University. Her research agenda targets talent management of school leaders in chronically low-performing and hard-to-staff school systems. She teaches courses related to human resource administration, introduction to educational administration, and K–12 instructional supervision. She also directs two national projects sponsored by the US Department of Education's Office of English Language Acquisition. Email: gimbert.1@osu.edu

Suzy Hardie is a clinical associate professor, the Master's and Education Specialist Program coordinator, and professional development school-district liaison at the University of South Carolina. Her research pertains to partnership development between universities and K–12 schools, retention of school leaders, and documentation of leadership during COVID-19 and beyond. Email: sehardie@mailbox.sc.edu

Dustin W. Miller is the director of the EdD in educational administration program and an assistant professor of clinical educational studies in the Department of Educational Studies at The Ohio State University. His research focuses on principal professional learning, leading in times of crises, and creating supportive LGBTQ+ environments for school leaders and teachers. He teaches courses on leadership, professional learning, and human resource management. Email: miller.1534@osu.edu

Rinice K. Sauls is a PhD student in the Educational Leadership and Policies Program at the University of South Carolina. Her research focuses on the experiences of Black women educational leaders in the workplace. She currently serves as the director of recruitment, retention, and evaluation in a South Carolina public school district. Email: rinicesauls@gmail.com

David Scanga is an adjunct professor at Saint Leo University in Florida, where he teaches various courses in educational leadership that prepare students for school administration. He received an EdD in educational leadership and policy studies from the University of South Florida. Dr. Scanga has been an active educator in the field for over forty years, working at home and overseas in private and public education settings. He has served students and families in roles that include school psychology, school administration, and assistant superintendent. His academic interests include school leadership, district leadership, and inclusion and diversity. He has co-authored several book chapters on systems thinking and networking to address the changing role of the school principal. Email: david.scanga@saintleo.edu

Renee Sedlack is an associate professor of educational leadership at Saint Leo University in Florida. She received an EdD in educational leadership and policy studies from the University of South Florida. Dr. Sedlack has forty-one years of experience in public education as a teacher, assistant principal, principal, and human resources director. Her focus as a school leader was to close the achievement gap for underserved populations and increase parent involvement in communities at the poverty level. Her research interest is how to close the achievement gap for underserved and incarcerated youth. She has presented at local and international conferences on a variety of subjects, including teacher recruitment and retention, classroom management, school safety, and leadership styles. Email: renee.sedlack@saintleo.edu

Haim Shaked serves as the president of Hemdat College of Education in Sdot Negev, Israel. As a scholar-practitioner with almost twenty years of experience as a school principal, Professor Shaked's research focuses on the principalship, in particular on instructional leadership and systems thinking in school leadership. He has published more than sixty peer-reviewed research articles, book chapters, edited books, and authored books on these topics. E-mail: haim.shaked@hemdat.ac.il; see also https://haimshaked.com/

Shmuel Shenhav is head of the Graduate School of Education at Michlalah Jerusalem College in Jerusalem, Israel; head of the Capstones Program for the training of school leaders in the Israel Ministry of Education; and head of the National-Religious Center for Leadership in Israel. He served as a school principal for many years. He is a national speaker on issues related to educational leadership and has published in journals such as the *International Journal of Educational Reform* and the *Journal of Practitioner Research*. Email: shenhav@huji.ac.il

Tammy S. Taylor is a PhD candidate, an elementary school principal in South Carolina Public Schools, and co-founder of Create and Educate, LLC. Her research pertains to the lived experiences of Black women, the Africana womanism paradigm, culture and climate in public schools, leadership styles, and the adultification of Black girls. Email: tammbo.taylor@gmail.com

Henry Tran is an associate professor at the University of South Carolina's Department of Educational Leadership and Policies. He studies issues related to human resources in education. He has published extensively on the topic, and holds two national human resources certifications. He is also the co-editor of the book *How Did We Get Here? The Decay of the Teaching Profession* (2022), editor of the *Journal of Education Human Resources*, and the director of the Talent Centered Education Leadership Initiative. Email: htr@sc.edu

www.ingramcontent.com/pod-product-compliance
Lightning Source LLC
Chambersburg PA
CBHW030656230426
43665CB00011B/1123